Andrew Murray at Keswick
and
Exeter Hall

By

Olea Nel

Clairvaux House

© Olea Nel 2021

Published by Clairvaux House

16/43 Clyde Street, Batemans Bay

Australia

ISBN 978-0-9876427-0-7 (e-book)

ISBN 978-0-9876427-1-4 (paperback)

Note

This book is a compilation of two previously published books: *Andrew Murray at Keswick: Three Unrevised Talks Given in 1895* which was published in November 2014, and *Andrew Murray at Exeter Hall: Three Talks on Prayer Given in 1895* which was published in October 2015.

While the texts and general introductions to these talks/ sermons are the same, I've also included a little-known testimony that Andrew Murray gave at Keswick in 1882, which does not appear in the original version of *Andrew Murray at Keswick*. I considered it essential to publish it in this two-book compilation because, like Andrew Murray's 1895 testimony, it was also given at Keswick, although at a time when he was an unknown pastor.

The importance of this 1882 testimony lies in the fact that he gave it a week after he was miraculously healed of a serious throat complaint while at the Bethshan Home of Faith healing. As an explanation was warranted, I've included one that appears immediately before this testimony.

***

Contents

Andrew Murray at Keswick

DERWENTWATER, FROM KESWICK.

*

Foreword

Andrew Murray is probably the best known South African devotional writer in the world to date. His first English publication *Abide in Christ* appeared in 1882. This was followed by other well-known works still avidly read today. By the time he was invited to speak at the Keswick Convention in the Lake District in 1895, he had published several more titles in English, including *Like Christ* (1884), *With Christ in the School of Prayer* (1885), *The New Life* (1885), *The Spirit of Christ* (1888) *Jesus Himself* (1893), *Be Perfect* (1893), and *The Holiest of All* (1894).

In short, by 1895 he had become one of the best known spiritual authors in Evangelical circles in the English-speaking world. It was therefore not surprising that he was invited to be one of the principal speakers at the Keswick Convention in 1895.

Andrew Murray's testimonies

I've included Andrew Murray's 1882 testimony at the beginning of this book because it sheds considerable light on his spiritual walk. He presented it at the Ministers Testimony

Meeting a week or so after the healing of his throat at the Bethshan Home of Faith Healing in London.

While the 1882 testimony is little known, his 1895 one appears in all his published biographies to date. Its significance lies in the fact that it was presented at Keswick by a mature, sixty-seven-year-old Andrew Murray, who had by then gained a greater understanding of his own spiritual journey, especially in relation to being filled with the Holy Spirit. As he, himself, explains, he did not experience the filling of the Spirit in a sudden way, nor on a specific occasion, but rather by slow increments over many years.

I have placed his 1895 testimony at the end of this book.

His three Keswick sermons given in 1895

What makes these three talks/sermons special is the fact that Andrew Murray never revised them for publication as he had done with most of the talks he delivered at other conventions that year. What usually happened was that the stenographer would write the sermon out, then give it to the speaker to revise before it appeared in the Convention newspaper. Having the full transcript, would also give the speaker the opportunity to publish the edited version as a chapter in a book. This was exactly what Andrew Murray had done with the talks he had delivered at other conventions and camp meetings.

All we know is that after presenting his final talk, he had needed to make a speedy departure for America to speak at the camp meetings there at the invitation of D.L. Moody. It appears that he did not have the notes of these talks with him, nor the stenographer's transcripts when he arrived in America. So during his tour, he prepared fresh sermons with different content that he delivered under the same titles as those at Keswick.

A good example of the difference between the Keswick and American sermons is the title "Carnal and Spiritual." At Keswick, this sermon was based on 1 Corinthians 3:1, whereas the American version, published in *The Deeper Christian Life*, is based on Luke 22:62, and bears little resemblance to the Keswick talk. The same holds true for the published sermon: "That God May Be All in All." It too is completely different from the Keswick one.

What is clear is that at the end of Andrew Murray's preaching tour, he endorsed the publication of the American sermons, while leaving the Keswick ones to sink into obscurity. But fortunately, you are able to read them here.

You have a treat in store.

To our knowledge, these Keswick talks are some of the few that exist that have not been revised or extensively edited for publication. They are ostensibly word for word as Andrew Murray delivered them.

I therefore invite you—in your mind's eye—to become one of the attendees at the Keswick Convention of 1895, and to imagine Andrew Murray preaching these sermons with light and shade and fiery exuberance. But before you do, here is a first-hand description of Andrew Murray that appeared in the British Weekly on 6 December 1894. It was penned by Rev. H.V. Taylor of Wellington with the view to introducing Andrew Murray to the Christian public of Britian prior to his arrival. A few of the more salient paragraphs are quoted below.

Andrew Murray's nature is profoundly devotional. He carries with him the atmosphere of prayer. He seems always wrapped about with a mantle of adoration. When preaching or conducting a service, his whole being is thrown into the task, and he glows with a fervency of spirit which seems impossible for human flesh to sustain.

The staid, venerable minister of the nineteenth century, with the sober, clerical garb and stiff white tie, which is de rigueur among the Dutch clergy, disappears, and an old Hebrew prophet stands before us—another Isaiah with his glowing imagery, a second Hosea with his plaintive, yearning appeals.

Audiences bend before the sweeping rain of his words like willows before a gale. The heart within the hearer is bowed, and the intellect awed. Andrew Murray's oratory is of the kind for which men willingly go into captivity.

***

Andrew Murray's 1882 Testimony

A few introductory remarks

This little-known testimony was given at the Ministers' Testimony Meeting on Saturday afternoon at the close of the Keswick Convention of 1882. It also appears in the October edition of *The Life of Faith* that year. I Included it at the beginning of this book because it is crucial to understanding Andrew Murray's spiritual breakthrough and the marked change in his life that followed.

To comprehend the significance of this testimony, I would like to introduce the following quotation made by Rev. Christiaan Rabie, who had been in Andrew Murray's confirmation class while a young teenager in Worcester, Western Cape, during the early 1860s. Rabie writes:

His pastoral visitation carried terror in the hearts of his parishioners. If his preaching was like thunderbolts from the summit of Sinai, what would personal rebuke be like? People felt, under the earnestness of his individual dealings, that they were being ground to powder.

But then Rabie adds:

I must add that there is a wide cleft between the stern Mr. Murray of those days and the loving and gentle Mr. Murray whom we knew in later years.

This sentiment was echoed by a female friend of the family in a letter to Andrew Murray's daughter Mary. She writes:

Do you remember the time when he was not allowed to preach? A great change came into his life after that. He used to be rather stern and very decided in his judgment of things. After that year, he was all love. His great humility also struck me forcibly at that time.

It is obvious from these quotations that there was a distinct 'before' and 'after' in Andrew Murray's ministry. The two years of silence spoken of here occurred between 1880 and 1882 when Murray was unable to preach due to a serious throat complaint.

So what provoked this marked change?

At first I thought it was solely due to the healing of his throat at the Bethshan Home of Faith Healing in London in July 1882. But on discovering this published testimony, I realized that the wonder of his healing proved to be only half the story. To understand it aright, we need to go back to 1862, just after the height of the Cape Revival. Although Andrew Murray had been an anointed and powerful preacher during the revival, by 1862, he had begun to lose the blessings gained and had begun to strive in his own strength again.

Anxious to get back on track, he had consecrated his life anew to the Lord, pleading to be filled with the Holy Spirit. But to his disappointment, this experience did not eventuate at the time. So he hung on in faith, claiming the promise that God would one day place His seal on his consecration by giving him the longed for experience of His palpable presence. Even after the miraculous healing of his throat at Bethshan in 1882, he still ached to receive the inflow of God's divine love.

A week after the healing of his throat, Andrew Murray attended the Keswick Convention of 1882. It was at an 'after meeting' on the second evening of the Convention that he finally received a fresh touch from the Lord. Thirteen years later, while giving his testimony at Keswick in 1895, he tells his audience that God had been giving him more and more of the Spirit, if he had only known it better. (See 1895 testimony.)

Needless to say, the explanation given above does not do justice to what actually occurred during Andrew Murray's consecration in 1862 and his determination to hang on in faith during the twenty years leading up to the healing of his throat and his breakthrough at Keswick in 1882. It goes without saying that the more you know of this story, the more you will realize how significant this testimony is for our understanding of his spiritual pilgrimage.

If you are interested in learning more, you can read the full story of Andrew Murray's walk with the Lord between 1860 and 1882 in my biographical novel on his life titled: ***Andrew Murray: from Spark to Flame,*** which is due out in 2021.

*

Andrew Murray's testimony published in *The Life of Faith*, October 1882

Let me sound a note of praise to the glory of our blessed Lord Jesus for what He has done for me here at Keswick. It is not that the teaching has been new to me. In the distant land in which I have been working, 6,000 miles away from here, I had some years ago learnt something of the blessed life of faith for myself, and been privileged to lead others to it. But there was still a longing for something more. And even of what I had experienced, the freshness and power got lost, the anointing with fresh oil was wanting. There was not that life in the perfect liberty and the continual clear leading of the Spirit in which the rest of faith was meant to be but the entrance. Self, seeking to do God's work—far more dangerous than refusing to obey—the flesh creeping in, learning spiritual truth and doing spiritual work rendered it impossible for the life of God to reveal its full power in the soul.

Affliction of the throat 1880-1882

Some two years ago it pleased the Lord to lay me aside from work by an affliction of the throat. In His good Providence I was brought to England some six weeks ago and led to the faith-healing home in London. I cannot say what a blessing my stay there has been to me. I was brought to see that while I only thought of healing as the first thing, and faith as the means to it, the Lord's purpose was to make the healing the secondary thing, the means to lead on to fuller faith and fellowship with Himself.

I was taught what an unspeakably solemn thing it was to ask the Lord to come and, by His Holy Spirit, to take possession of the body as its health and strength. I saw how this could not be without a searching out and casting out of self as I had never understood before; an acknowledgement of Christ's claim on the body, and an entire surrender of body, soul and spirit to His service.

Such a surrender was God's purpose in the sickness, and it was only as such a surrender was made that the healing could be given, or faith rise to receive it. All this I was led to see and thank God for. And yet it was as if the surrender I had made, and the faith in which I had accepted Christ, not only as my Healer, but as the Power of an entirely new life was still wanting its divine seal. I was holding fast to the promise, but without the joy and love which must in due time follow.

During 'after-meetings' at Keswick

On Tuesday evening at the after-meeting, I rose with others to testify my desire, but could not rise a second time with those who could testify that they had realized that Christ was to them what they had believed. It was as if I only felt how utterly helpless every effort to grasp the blessing is, and could do nothing but bow in emptiness before the Lord.

On Wednesday evening I was again in the after-meeting, and it was there the Lord revealed Himself. And as the words of the simple chorus were sung—"wonderful cleansing, wonderful filling, wonderful keeping"—I saw it all: Jesus cleansing, Jesus filling, Jesus keeping.

The power of the blood of Christ

I had for a year back been seeing what wonderful things God's Word says about the power of the blood of Christ. It was *"through the blood"* that the God of peace brought again from the dead our Lord Jesus. It was *by His own blood* He entered into the Holy Place. It was with the blood of the better sacrifice that the heavenly things themselves were purged. It was thus through the blood that the power of sin and death had been overcome; through the blood alone that Christ had obtained and could hold His place in heaven as our Mediator. The blood that had obtained such mighty victories in the kingdom of sin and hell, and in the kingdom of heaven, too. Surely that blood that could cleanse the soul is a power too little known.

I believed and received Jesus as my Cleanser.

Jesus' cleansing, filling, keeping

I look to Him to make the blood-sprinkling as glorious and effectual as the blood-shedding was. And I saw that the filling cannot but follow the cleansing. The vessel He hath cleansed He will not leave empty; the temple He hath cleansed, He will fill with the glory, as it is written, "The glory of the Lord filled the house of the Lord." And thus what He has cleansed and filled He cannot but keep, and certainly will use. It is far too precious in His sight. For what He does to souls He not only does because it is His work given Him by the Father, but because He loves them as Himself. He not only gives a blessing in what He does. He gives Himself.

And now, since I yesterday heard the words of that beautiful chorus, it is as if they are continually whispering within me:

Precious, gentle, holy Jesus!
Blessed Bridegroom of my heart,
In thy secret inner chamber,
Thou wilt show me what Thou art.

I could say more, but this is enough just to give my grateful testimony to the love of our blessed Lord, and what He has done for me at Keswick. Let us all, my beloved brothers and sisters, seek to know and trust this blessed Jesus. Let Him— Jesus' cleansing, filling, keeping—be to us all in all, and let us have no desire but to live to the glory of His blessed Name. God grant that it may be so.

***

Three Sermons given

at the

Keswick Convention

of 1895

Sermon 1: Carnal and Spiritual

You will find the words from which I want to speak to you in 1 Corinthians 3:1: "And I brethren, could not speak unto you as unto spiritual, but as unto carnal, even as unto babes in Christ."

The Apostle commences the chapter by telling these Corinthians that there are two stages of Christian experience. Some Christians are *carnal*, some are *spiritual*. By the discernment which God's Spirit gave the Apostle, he saw that the Corinthians were carnal, and he wanted to tell them so. You will find the word carnal four times in these verses.

The Apostle felt that all his preaching would do no good if he talked about spiritual things to men who were unspiritual. They were Christians, real Christians, babes in Christ; but there was one deadly fault—they were *carnal*. So the Apostle seems to say, "I cannot teach you spiritual truth about the spiritual life; you cannot take it in. But that was not because they were stupid. They were very clever, full of knowledge, but were unable to understand spiritual teaching.

That teaches us this simple lesson—that all the trouble in the Church of Christ among Christians who sometimes get a blessing and lose it again, is just because they are *carnal*, and all that we need if we want to keep the blessing is that we become *spiritual.* We must choose what style of spiritual life we would like to live—the carnal life, or the spiritual. Choose the spiritual, and God will be delighted to give it to you. O God help us all to say tonight, "Lord, make me a spiritual man. Fill me with Thy Spirit."

Now, if we are to understand this teaching, we must begin by trying thoroughly to know what the carnal state is, and I think I shall be able to point you to four very marked characteristics of the carnal state.

The first thing I have to say about it is that the Carnal State is a state of protracted infancy.

It is a time ago since you were converted, and you ought to have been a young man by this time, but you are still a babe in Christ. "I have fed you with milk and not with meat; for hitherto ye were not able to bear it."

You know what a babe is and what a beautiful thing babyhood is. You cannot have a more beautiful thing than a child six months old with its ruddy cheeks, its laughing and smiling face, the kicking of its little feet and the movement of its little fingers. What a beautiful object! But suppose I saw such a child and came back after six months and the child was not a bit bigger, the parents would begin to say, "We are afraid there is something the matter. The child won't grow." And if after three years I came back and saw there the baby no bigger yet, I should find the parents sad. They would tell me, "The doctor says there's some terrible disease about the child; it cannot grow. He says it is a wonder it is alive, and yet it does live." I come back after ten years and there is that helpless infant and still there is no growth.

You see, babyhood at the proper time is the most beautiful thing in the world, but babyhood continued too long is a burden and sorrow, a sign of disease. And that was the state of many of those Corinthian Christians. They continued babies.

Now, what are the marks of a babe? There are especially two marks: a babe cannot help itself, and a babe cannot help others.

A babe cannot help itself, and that is the life of many Christians. They make their ministers spiritual nurses of babes. It is a solemn thing that these spiritual babes keep their ministers occupied all the time in nursing them and feeding them, and they never want to grow to be men, and they never help themselves. They do not know how to feed themselves on Christ's Word, and the minister must feed them. They do not know what contact with God is, and the minister must pray for them. They do not know what it is to live as those who have God to help them. They always want to be nursed. Do take care that *that* does not become the reason why *you* come to the Convention.

But oh, you know what baby does? Baby always keeps the house going and very often mother cannot go out because there is a baby, or the servant must be there to keep the baby, or the nurse must be there; but baby always occupies somebody. You cannot leave him alone. So there are many spiritual infants to whom ministers are always going and who are always wanting some help. Instead of allowing them to be trained up to know their God and be strong, alas! It is a protracted infancy. They cannot help themselves, but occupy others.

Is not that just what we read in the Epistle to the Hebrews? There was the very same condition. We read that those who had been so long converted, and who ought to have been teachers, needed themselves to be taught the very rudiments of Christianity. And there are, as I have said, people who are always wanting to be helped instead of being a help to others. For a little child, a spiritual babe of three months old, to be carnal and not know altogether what sin is, and not yet to have got victory, is, as Paul said, a thing not to be wondered at. But when a man continues year after year in the same state of always being conquered by sin, there is something radically wrong. Nothing can keep a child in protracted infancy except disease of some sort. And if we have to say continually, "I'm not spiritual," then do let us say, "O God I am carnal; I am in a diseased state and want to be helped out of it."

The second mark of a carnal state is that sin and failure prove master

Sin has the upper hand. What proof does Paul give that those people were carnal? He first charges them, and then he asks them a question. "Among you, there is envying and strife and divisions. Are ye not carnal?" And then again one says, "I am of Paul," and another, "I am of Apollos," and another, "I am of Cephas." "Are you not carnal?" asks Paul, in effect. Is not that evident? You just act like other men. You are not acting like heavenly, renewed men who live in the power and love of the Holy Ghost.

Oh, friends, you know that God who loveth us dwelleth in light, and that love is the great commandment, and that of the Cross of Christ is the evidence of God's love, and that the first fruit of the Holy Spirit is love. The whole of John's Gospel means *love*, and when men give way to their tempers and pride and envying and divisions; when you hear people saying sharp things about others; when a man cannot open out his whole heart and face a brother who has done him wrong and forgive him; when a woman can speak about her neighbor with contempt as "that wretched thing," or say to another, "Oh, how I dislike that woman"—all these are fruits of the carnal spirit. Every touch of unlovingness is nothing but the *flesh*.

Most of you know that the word *carnal* is a form of the Latin word for *flesh*, and all unlovingness is nothing but the fruit or work of the flesh. The flesh is selfish and proud and unloving. Therefore every sin against love is nothing but the proof that the man is carnal.

You say, "I have tried to conquer it, but I cannot." That is what I want to impress upon you. Do not try while you are in the carnal state to bear spiritual fruit. You must have the Holy Spirit in order to love God, and then the carnal will be conquered. He will give you the Spirit to do the right. And it is not only true of the sins against love, but there are so many other sins. Take worldliness, which somebody says has "honeycombed the Church." Take the love of money, take the pursuit of business, making people sacrifice everything to the increase of riches. Take so much of our life: the seeking after luxury and pleasure and position. What is all that but the flesh? It gratifies the flesh. It is exactly what the world thinks desirable and delights in. And if you live like the world, it is proof that the spirit of the world, which is in the flesh, is in you. The carnal state is proved by the power of sin.

Somebody asked me yesterday, or the day before, "How about the want of love of prayer?" He wanted to know how the art of loving fellowship with God could be attained. I said, "My brother, that cannot be attained in any way until you discover that it must come outside of the carnal state. The flesh cannot delight in God. That is your difficulty. You must not say or write down a resolution in your journal that "I will pray more." You cannot force it. But let the axe come to the root of the tree. Cut down the carnal mind. How can you cut it down? *You* cannot, but let the Holy Spirit of God come with the condemnation of sin and the Cross of Christ. Give over the flesh to death, and the Spirit of God will come in. And then you will learn to love prayer and love God and love your neighbor. And you will be possessed of humility and spirit-mindedness and heavenly mindedness. *The carnal state is the root of every sin.*

I come to the next point. If we want to know this carnal state thoroughly, we must take very special notice that the carnal state can co-exist with great spiritual gifts.

Remember, there is a great difference between spiritual gifts and spiritual graces, and that is what many people do not understand. Among the Corinthians, for instance, there were very wonderful spiritual gifts. In the first chapter Paul says, "*I thank my God . . . that ye are enriched in all utterance and in all knowledge.*" That was something wonderful to praise God for. And in the second Epistle he says in effect, "You do not come behind in any gift. See that you have the gift of liberality also." And in the twelfth chapter, how he speaks about the gifts of prophecy and the faith that could remove mountains, and of knowledge, and of all mysteries as things that they were ardently seeking for. But he tells them these will not profit them without them having *love*. They delighted in the gifts and did not care for the graces. But Paul shows them a more excellent way—to learn to love and to be humble; that love is the greatest thing of all, for love is God-like above everything.

It is a very solemn thing for us to remember that a man may be gifted with prophecy; that a man may be a faithful and successful worker in some particular sphere among the poor and needy, and yet that by the sharpness of his judgment and the pride that comes into him, and by other things, he may give proof that while his spiritual gifts are wonderful, spiritual graces are too often absent.

Oh, take care that Satan does not deceive one of us with the thought, "But I work for God and God blesses me, and others look up to me, and I am the means of helping others." Beloved, fellow Christian, that **a carnal man may have spiritual gifts** is unspeakably solemn, because it must bring the most earnest and successful man to his knees before God with the thought, "Am I not—after all that God's Spirit works in me as a matter of gift—possibly giving way to the flesh, in lack of humility, or love, or purity or holiness? God search us and try us for His name's sake.

A further point is this: The carnal state renders it impossible for a man to receive spiritual truth.

This is of the utmost importance here at Keswick. You see perhaps hundreds of Christians hungering for the Word, and they listen and they say, "What beautiful truths, what clear doctrines, what helpful expositions of God's Word!" And yet they do not get helped one step; or they get helped for two or three weeks and the blessing passes away. What is the reason? There is an evil at the bottom: the carnal state is hindering the reception of spiritual truth.

A am afraid that in our churches we often make a terrible mistake. We preach to carnal Christians what is only fit for spiritual men, and they think it is so beautiful, and they take it into their heads and delight in it and say, "That is grand. What a view of the truth that man can give!" Yet their lives remain unchanged. They are carnal with all the spiritual teaching they get.

If there is one thing that we ought each to ask God at this Convention it is this: "Lord deliver me from taking up spiritual teaching into a carnal mind." The only evidence that you get a blessing at Keswick is that you are lifted out of the carnal into the spiritual state. God is willing to do it, and let us plead for it and accept it.

So much for the meaning of carnal.

Now comes a very important and solemn question: Is it possible for a man to get out of the carnal and into the spiritual state? And how is it possible?

I want to answer that, and point out the steps that must be taken to that end. I have asked God that He may help me to speak as simply as to little children, for I want to say to every honest, earnest heart that is longing to be spiritual, you can get out of the carnal state tonight into the spiritual state. And what is needed for that?

I think the first thing needed is that *a man must have some sight of the spiritual life and some faith in it.* At bottom, our hearts are so full of unbelief—without our knowing it—that we do not accept, as a settled matter, that we can become spiritual men tonight. We do not believe it.

I heard a most interesting story just before I left the Cape. I was talking to a man of much Christian experience about my coming over to England, and I said to him, "Tell me, what is the state of the Christians in England? You have worked among them and know them well." He replied, "I believe there is nothing so terrible amongst them as *unbelief.*" Then he told me a story of a young man of high promise and great gifts who was in England working for Christ. That young man had great gifts, but my friend could not understand why, with all those gifts, he did not get more blessing.

Well, these two men spent a whole day trying to find out what it was that was hindering the younger of them from being a greater blessing. The person to whom I spoke told me that his friend had to take a meeting that same night, but that he could not go to it as he felt so feeble, and the power of the world so strong. He was not assured that God was ready to give the blessing. So the other said, "I will take your meeting. Go home and come back tomorrow morning at nine o'clock." He came back the next morning, and they began to speak and pray again, and in the course of the day, the young man received a blessing from God. And since that time he has been ten times more blessed in his work than ever before. Oh! Do believe that if you are ready and willing it is possible for God to make a spiritual man of you. And try and just get a vision of the spiritual life.

What is that vision? You know the word speaks about two powers of life: the *flesh* and the *Spirit*—the flesh, our life under the power of sin; the Spirit, God's life coming to take the place of our life.

Some people have said to me with respect to what I have already spoken about the *death of self*, "Oh, this is so hard to understand. Do tell us what it is?" I replied, "Do not try to understand it with your intellect. The death is in Him. He died for you and he will give it to you if you yield yourselves utterly to Him." What we need and what the Bible tells us is to give our whole life—with every idea of strength or power—away unto death and to become nothing, and receive the life of Christ and of the Spirit to do all for us. Do believe that can be.

You say, "That is so high and holy, and glorious, I do not think I can reach it." No, *you* cannot, but **God** will send it down to you. Your reaching up is the great danger. You cannot reach it, but if you believe that God wants—in a supernatural way, according to his everlasting love—to give you down from heaven the power of the Holy Spirit, then God will do for you more than you can ask or think. Let that be the first step we take tonight.

I do believe that it is possible for a man to live every day as led by the Holy Ghost. I have read in God's Word that as many as are led by the Spirit, they are the children of God. I have read in God's Word that if we are born again, we are to walk by the Spirit or in the Spirit.

Dear friends, it *is* possible. It is the life God calls you to, and that Christ redeemed you for. As soon as He shed His blood, He went away to heaven to send the Spirit to his people. As soon as He was glorified, His first work was to give the Holy

Spirit. If you begin to believe in the power of Christ's blood to cleanse you, and in the power of the glorified Christ to give you His Spirit in your heart, you have taken the first step in the right direction. Though you should feel ever so wretched, do hold fast in Jesus. He can fill you with the Spirit, for He has commanded you to be filled with the Spirit. Will you come tonight and say, "God helping me, I want to be a spiritual man."

But secondly, it is not enough that a man should have a vision of the spiritual life which is to be lived; it is also very needful that a man should be really convicted of his carnality.

This is difficult and solemn, but as I say, a needful lesson. There is a great difference—I do want to help you—between the sins of the unconverted man and the sins of the believer. As an unconverted man, you had to be convicted of sin and make confession of it; you all admit that. But what were you convicted of chiefly? Of the grossness of sin, and very much of the guilt and punishment of sin. But there was very little conviction of inward spiritual sins. You had no knowledge of them. There was very little conviction of inward sinfulness. God does not always give that ordinarily in conversion.

And so how is a man to get rid of these two things: the vile sin and the deep inner sinfulness? In this way: After he has become a Christian, God gives the Holy Spirit to convict him of the carnal, fleshly life, and then the man begins to mourn over it, and be ashamed of it, and cry out like Paul, "O wretched man that I am! I am a believer, but who shall deliver me from the body of this death?" He begins to turn around for help and to ask, "Where am I to get deliverance?" He seeks it in many ways: by struggling and resolve; but he does not get it until he is brought to cast himself absolutely at the feet of Jesus. Do not forget that if you are to become a spiritual man, if you are to be filled with the Holy Ghost, it must come from God in heaven who alone can do it.

How different our living and praying and preaching would be if the presence of the holy One, who fills Eternity, who fills the universe, were revealed to us! To that end, God wants to bring us to a condition of utter brokenness.

Somebody said to me, "It is dreadful, that call to *die*." Yes, it is dreadful if you had to do it in your own strength. But oh, if you would only understand that God gave Jesus to die, and Jesus did it all, and God wants to plant you into Jesus that you may be delivered from the accursed power of the flesh. Oh! Do believe that it is a blessing to be utterly broken down and utterly in despair, that you may learn to trust in God alone. Paul says somewhere in effect, "I had the sentence of death in myself that I might learn not to trust in myself, but in God who raiseth the dead." That is the place you must come to under the conviction of your carnality—"the flesh prevails and triumphs in me, and I cannot conquer it. Have mercy my God! God help me!" And God *will*. Oh! Become willing to bow before God in conviction and confession.

And then comes the third thing: That is to believe that we can pass from the carnal to the spiritual condition in one moment of time.

People want to grow out of the carnal into the spiritual, and they never can. They seek more preaching and teaching in order, as they think, to grow out of the carnal into the spiritual. That babe that I spoke of, though ten years old, remained as big as a child of six months; it had got disease, and it wanted healing. Then growth would come. Now, the carnal state is a state of terrible disease. The carnal Christian is a babe in Christ. He is a child of God, Paul says, but he has this terrible disease and consequently he cannot grow.

How is the healing to come? It must come through God, and God longs to give it to you this very hour.

Let me say here that a man who becomes a spiritual man tonight is not yet a man of spiritual maturity. I cannot expect from a young Christian who has got the Holy Spirit in His fullness, what I can expect from a mature Christian who has been filled with Him for twenty years. There is a great deal of growth and maturity in the spiritual life. But what I speak of, when I speak of *one step* is this: you can change your place and, instead of standing in the carnal life, enter the spiritual life.

Note the reason why the two expressions are used. In the carnal man there is something of the spiritual nature; but you know the bodies get their names from that which is their most prominent element. A thing may be used for two or three objects, but it will likely get its name from that which is the most prominent. A thing may have several characteristics, but the name will be given according to that which is most striking. So, Paul says, in other words, to those Corinthians, "You babes in Christ are carnal, you are under the power of the flesh, giving way to temper and unloveliness and not growing or capable of receiving spiritual truth with all your gifts."

And the spiritual man is a man *who has not reached final perfection;* there is abundant room to grow. But if you look at him, the chief mark of his nature and conduct is that he is a man given up to the Spirit of God. He is not perfect, but he is a man who has taken up the right position, and said, "Lord God, I have given myself to be led by Thy Spirit. Thou has accepted me and blessed me and the Holy Spirit now leads me." Do let us get hold of the thought that, God helping us, we can tonight leave our place on the one side, and take it on the other.

You may have heard the story that is often used in evangelical services about the man who was converted by a minister drawing a line and talking to him about it. He was a sick man, seventy years of age, and a minister visited him faithfully, and talked to him about the blood of Christ. "Oh yes," responded the man, "I know about the blood of Christ, that it can save us, and about pardon, and that if God does not pardon us we cannot enter heaven." Yet the minister saw that the man had not the slightest sense of sin. Whatever the minister said, he said "Yes" to, and there was no life in it, no conviction of sin.

And the minister tells that when he himself was beginning to get into despair, he one day prayed, "Oh God, help me to show this man his state." All at once a thought came into his mind. The floor of the man's room was strewn with sand, and on the one side he wrote the words, "Sin", "Death," "Hell," and on the other side, "Christ," "Life," "Heaven." The old man asked, "What are you doing?" The minister answered, "Listen! Do you think one of these letters on the left side could get up and go over the line to the right side?" "Of course not," was the answer. Then the minister said solemnly, "Just as little can a sinner who is on the left side get over to the right side. That line divides all mankind, and those who are saved are on the right side. It is Christ who must take you up from the left side and bring you to the right side. On what side are you?" There was no answer. The minister prayed with him, and went home praying that God would bless him. He went back next day, and the question was, "Well my friend, on what side are you?" He at once answered with a sigh, "On the wrong side." But it was not long before the man welcomed the Gospel and accepted Christ.

I would like tonight to draw a line straight through the center of this hall and ask all of you who believe and confess that God has given you His Holy Spirit to lead you, and who know what the joy of the Holy Spirit is, to take your places at the right-hand side. Then I would ask all of you who have felt tonight that you are still carnal to come to the left side and say, "Oh God, I must confess that my Christian life is for the most part carnal, under the power of the flesh." Then I would plead with you, and tell you that you cannot save yourself from the flesh or get rid of it., but that if you come and accept Christ afresh tonight, Christ can lift you over into the new life. You belong to Christ and He belongs to you. But what you need is just to cast yourself upon Him, and He will reveal the power of His crucifixion in you, to give you victory over the flesh. Cast yourselves, with the confession of sin, and with utter helplessness, at the feet of the lamb of God. He can give you deliverance.

That brings me to my last thought. The first was: a man must see the spiritual life; the second: a man must be convicted of and confess his carnal condition; the third: a man must see that it is but one step from the one to the other.

And then lastly, he must take the decisive step, and he must do so in the faith that Christ is able to keep him.

Yes, it is not a mere view, it is not a consecration in any sense of its being in our power; it is not a surrender by the strength of our will. No! These are elements that may be present. But the great thing is that we must look to Christ to keep us tomorrow, and the next day, and always. We must get the life of God within us. Yes, we want a life that will stand against any temptation, a life that will last not only till another Keswick, but till death.

We want by the grace of God to experience what the almighty indwelling and saving power of Christ can do for us. Oh, God is waiting, Christ is waiting, the Holy Spirit is waiting. Do not you see what has been wrong, and why it is you have been wandering in the wilderness? Do not you see the good land, the land of promise, in which God is going to keep and bless you?

Oh, remember the story of Caleb and Joshua and the spies. Ten men said in effect, "We never can conquer those people." And two said, "We are able, for God has promised." Step out tonight upon the promises of God. Listen to God's Word: "The law of the spirit of life in Jesus Christ hath made me free from the law of sin and death." Take a word like that and claim that God shall do for you through His Holy Spirit what He has offered you.

Come tonight and never mind though there be no new experience, and no feeling, and no excitement, and no light, but apparently darkness. Come and stand upon the Word of God, the everlasting God. God promises as Father His Holy Spirit to every hungering child. Will He then not give it to you? How shall He not give the Holy Spirit to them that ask Him? How could He not do it?

Brethren, as truly as Christ was given for you on Calvary, and you have believed in the blood, so truly the Holy Spirit has been given for you and me. Open your hearts tonight and be "filled with the Spirit." Come and trust the blood of Christ for the cleansing, confess the carnality of every sin, and cast it into the fountain of the blood, and then believe in the living Christ to bless you with the blessing of His Spirit.

Sweet Childhood of eternal life!
Whilst troubled days and years go by,
In stillness hushed from stir and strife,
Within thy arms I lie.

It is easy for the lamb to be gentle, and for the mother to love her child because it is their very nature. We never can love as God wants us to till it becomes our nature to love. Thank God, His love is able to possess us. Let it enter into our hearts and dwell there, then we shall be able to love even the unlovely and the unlovable.

*

Sermon 2: The Way to the Higher Life

The words I which to speak to you, you will find in the Gospel according to St. Mark, the tenth chapter from the thirty-fifth verse: "*And James and John the sons of Zebedee, come unto Him, saying Master, we would that Thou shouldest do for us whatsoever we desire.*"

It looks very bold, but they remembered that those were the words that Christ had used, and so they avail themselves of his promise. "And He said unto them, 'What would ye that I should do for you?' They said unto Him, '*Grant unto us that we may sit one on thy right hand, and the other on Thy left hand, in Thy glory.*'"

This last verse gives us our subject this evening: The Way to the Higher Life.

Here we have two men asking for a place on the throne of glory. And we have our blessed Jesus teaching us what the real way is to the higher life. Oh let us all yield ourselves to His teaching and every heart say, "Blessed Lord, teach me tonight!"

Or, I might give as the subject of my address: *The Path of Consecration*. We talk so much about it. Let us tonight study in the words of Jesus and in His presence, what the path of consecration is.

And our first thought is this: The blessing which consecration seeks.

What is that? You cannot find it put more beautifully than in the words of the Bible: "Grant unto us that we may sit . . . on thy right hand . . . in Thy glory." Three things they ask: *Nearness to Jesus; Likeness to Jesus; Power for Jesus.*

Nearness to Jesus. Is not that what your heart longs for when you talk of consecration? Oh, if I could only be having Him all the time for me, always near, and be every day conscious of His presence!

And more; they desired not only nearness to Jesus—to be with Him on the throne—but likeness to Jesus. This is not beyond His heart. He has promised it.

But they asked not only for nearness and likeness to Jesus, but for *the very power of Jesus* that they may use it for Him. What a blessed answer it was that they gave Jesus! It meant more than they knew. There were elements in it that were not good, but what a large answer it was to the Savior's request: "What would ye that I should do for you?"

And Christ comes tonight to every one of us with the same question, and the teaching of the last three days has all been meant by Him to help you answer it. Come now tonight and formulate your petition and tell Jesus what you want. Are you ready to whisper up to Jesus as your answer: "Lord, perfect nearness to Thee; Lord perfect likeness to thee; Lord perfect power for service for Thee?" Is that your heart? Are you content with the groveling life of a man who is only just saved, who is just a Christian and nothing more? Or, do you want to aim at the very highest? Do so my brother, and I pray God to give it you.

And now, as to the second point. The first is the blessing that consecration seeks. The next is the mistakes that consecration makes.

Jesus says at once, "*Ye know not what ye ask.*" Yes, this petition of the disciples was an ignorant one. And oh, remember that in our prayers and consecration there are often terrible mistakes and such ignorance. But it is ever our comfort to know that Jesus spoke very kindly and tenderly to those disciples, and that for our ignorance and errors, He will not cast us off.

What were their mistakes? One was that they were asking for the fruit, and the root had not been planted. They were looking above, and Christ said as it were, "Look downward; I must have the root."

A child sometimes plants a branch with beautiful fruit upon it at the seaside, in the sand, and makes a garden. And we are always wanting only the fruit and the blessing, but Christ wants us to have the root deep down.

Another mistake was this: They did not remember that what they wanted was not His to give. He had not the position to give it. The Father alone could give it to them who were prepared for it, and for whom it was prepared. How careful Christ is to honor the Father. He wants to bring us to God. He took great trouble to draw the disciples to believe in himself, but he took infinite trouble to say, in other words, "I am only here to take you up to God."

May we all learn that Christ says, "It is the Father that has got the blessing, and you must go to Him through Me." Some people think that if we talk too much of God, Christ will lose His place. Brethren, Christ will become doubly precious, for the more I long for heaven, the more I find I cannot get there without Christ. God help us to seek God in Christ.

And there was still more ignorance. They did not know that their desire for glory was carnal. It was mixed up with the idea of a temporal kingdom, and therefore the Savior said, in effect, "You do not know what you are talking about." Further, there was selfishness in it. They wanted to have the best places and be above the other disciples. "My disciples, you do not know what you ask."

And dear friends, just at the time when one is dealing more earnestly with souls about salvation, one wants to say, "Remember, you do not understand it all." One dear sister said very earnestly yesterday, "Explain to me what it really means, that dying in Christ." And another spoke to me today about being filled with the Spirit. I have so often to say to such, "Do not try to understand it perfectly, but go in your darkness and ask for something beyond what you can understand, and then let God deal with you in the glory of His love."

Confess your ignorance and say, Oh God, this thing is too great, I cannot comprehend it, but I will trust Thee for it."

Oh! The mistakes we make in our consecration! There is often selfishness, and there is often pride, and there is often carnal apprehension and the desire for being very happy and holy and useful; and *self* is at the bottom of it.

Now Christ does not want His disciples to be deluded by an unsatisfactory consecration. And He helped them.

And that brings us to the next point: the consecration that Christ demands.

"Ye know not what ye ask. Can ye drink of the cup that I drink of, and be baptized with the baptism that I am baptized with?" This is the consecration which Christ asks as the path to the higher life.

Think what it means. What is the cup? You know that refers to Gethsemane. And what was the cup concerning which He asked the Father that it might be taken away?

You know that if you study your Bible, the Bible speaks only of two cups: *the cup of wrath and the cup of blessing.* The cup of the wrath of God, and the cup of blessing and thanksgiving. Which cup was it respecting which Christ had to say, *"Father, if it be possible, let this cup pass from me?"* It was the cup of wrath on account of our sins—that accursed death upon the tree of Calvary. But oh, thank God! He drank it, and He comes now to give it to us to drink; but the curse is out of it.

And what is it to us? Nothing but this: You know what Gethsemane means—the surrender of the will. That is the cup. It cost Him a struggle to say, in other words, "Thy will shall be done. I will drink it up." But he conquered. And Jesus comes and says to us too, *"Can ye drink the cup that I drink of, and be baptized with the baptism that I am baptized with?"*

You know what that means? Did not He say, speaking of His death, "I have a baptism to be baptized with, and how am I straightened till it be accomplished? He felt long before the agony in His soul that was Calvary. That was the Cross. That was his baptism. And He asks the disciples, *"Can ye . . . be baptized with the baptism that I am baptized with?"*

Christians, you want the higher life, you want the glory, and you want the nearness and likeness and power of your Lord, but He asks you tonight, "Can you drink my cup and are you willing to be baptized with my baptism?

Do remember that there is no path to the glory but through death. Why is it that some Christians are unwilling to surrender themselves to it? Because they do not see the need of it. They do not see that it is a righteous sentence that sinful nature should be condemned to death, and that, in the very nature of things, it is an absolute necessity that, in order to get rid of their life, they must die before God's life can come in.

Someone said to me yesterday, when talking of these things, "And must we then die every day?" As if the thought was, "is it not enough to die once for all with Jesus in order to live the resurrection life? My brother, would that I could help you to see that the death of Christ is a thing for every day as really as His life is. They are inseparable.

I cannot make it plainer than by pointing you to some splendid oak tree. Where was that oak born? In a grave. The acorn was pushed under the ground. It had its grave there, and in that grave it sprouted and sent its buds upwards. And the tree—I ask you—was it only one day that it stood in the grave?" No! That oak for a hundred years has stood every day in the grave, in that place of death. And in that place of death it has found its life and beauty.

And so, let us learn the lesson that death and resurrection are inseparably combined. You cannot get the resurrection life anywhere, or live it, or enjoy it, except in the grave of Jesus. But as that oak tree spreads its dark roots under the cold, black soil every year, farther and farther, and lives in the grave, so the stem and the branches and the leaves come upward into the sunshine; and it is the reward of the roots down in the grave that the tree is so beautiful and so bright in God's creation. I pray you to learn that it is not a transaction once for all. No!

Bless God! There is a divine beginning, a glorious sudden beginning when God opens our eyes, and we have seen the crucified one as our life, and counted ourselves dead because we see we are dead in Christ. But let that be the disposition of every day: dead to the world, dead to sin, dead to self, dead to all that is not God's. That is the grave out of which the glorious life of resurrection, joy and power shall grow. And I come with the question tonight: Can you be baptized—can you bear it, are you willing for it—with the baptism with which Jesus was baptized? There was for Him, as the Apostle and High Priest of our profession, no gate to God or to heaven but through death. And there is no gate for us but in the crucified One and in fellowship with Him.

Now comes our next point: What was the answer of these disciples? There you have: The consecration yielded.

They answered, "We can." Simple disciples! They little knew what these words meant. Yet, blessed be God! *Jesus accepted their consecration.* For what was His answer? Look at its fullness and tenderness. *"Jesus said unto them, Ye shall indeed drink of the cup that I drink of; and with the baptism that I am baptized with shall ye be baptized."* Oh! Do you not love this tender Redeemer? There were those poor, foolish disciples saying to Him that they could drink that cup. And yet they knew nothing about what it was going to be, and that they could be baptized with His baptism, and yet they did not understand it.

And how did they carry out their vow? All the eleven on the last night "*forsook Him and fled.*" And at the very supper table they were quarrelling again about who was chief. How they misunderstood and grieved, and at last forsook Him! But, thank God, Jesus accepted that consecration.

But how could He do it if it was so untrue? At bottom it was true. The heart was right. They clung to Him. It just meant this: "Lord we are ready for anything;" and in his loving heart He seemed to say, "I know you are."

And dear friends, if I come to you with the question, "Can you be baptized with the baptism that He was baptized with?" can you say, "Jesus I will live as a crucified one in Thee; Jesus I will follow Thee to Calvary; I will not rest until my life is spent in the fellowship of the cross"? Are you ready to give the answer: "We can"?

I know you tremble—and it is right you should. In the light we have in this text, it is not wrong if we say, "*Lord I cannot, I am impotent.*" But rather say, "Lord in *Thy strength* I can. In *Thy strength* I will drink thy cup and will be baptized with Thy baptism." Then, when you leave this meeting or Keswick for home, get with Jesus and sign your covenant: "Thy cup, O lamb of God is my cup. Thy baptism is my baptism." Jesus will carry you through it. His kind answer to those disciples meant more than this—"Oh yes, foolish children, you do not know what you say, but you mean it. I know how your vows will fail, but I will take it from you." That was not so much His meaning. He had another thought: "Yes my disciples you shall. I will carry you through it all, and lead you from Gethsemane and Calvary onward to Pentecost."

Beloved, come tonight and make yourselves ready. Prepare yourselves for that word: "We can." That is consecration. "We can in *Thy strength*." Oh! What joy there would be in heaven tonight if this great company were to fall down and say, when Jesus asks, "Can ye drink the cup, can ye be baptized into my death?" "Yes Lord we can." Let our hearts even now say it.

And what comes next? Something very interesting. Our fourth point was the consecration yielded by them and accepted by Christ. Now comes: The contention of the disciples about it.

Is it not a very terrible thing that every higher life movement awakens contention and division? Here are these two disciples. Their hearts are for Jesus and their longings are for glory, and it was not unnatural that they should say—for they had been his special friends—"Lord, give us a place on thy throne." But there are the other disciples, and how quick they are to condemn the two! They do not know that in doing so they are revealing, by the jealousy of their own hearts, that they are just as unfit for the throne as James and John.

And let me say, Keswick lifts up the standard of holiness, but if there is one thing that is heavy on my heart during my stay in England, it is that God's children in England are not as near each other as they should be. Oh brethren, is not it a terrible thing that this holiness banner is becoming a mark of separation, and that there are people who say, "Yes this is right," and "That is right," and "This is wrong" and "That is wrong," and unconsciously there comes a separation. I pray you, call upon God very fervently and unitedly that He will pour out such a spirit of love on His people in England that they cannot help coming together.

I do not want them to compromise truth or disguise their differences, but I want them to come together and say, "O, God we are one, and we want to show it to each other." In the Spirit of love we want to say, "We shall bear with your differences, even when we think them wrong, but *one* we are." God grant that the power of holiness may come among us and that the spirit of those disciples may pass away from us. God grant that the spirit of Jesus the crucified, and His love may fill us with devotion, not only to the heathen and the unconverted, but to our brethren who are near to us in Christ Jesus, though separated for a little while by earthly distinctions.

And then comes the next thought, and that leads us still deeper down. We read: "But Jesus called them to him."

The Lord Jesus cannot bear division; it grieves him terribly. You know how He said, in effect, "This is to be a mark that ye are my disciples: that ye love one another as I have loved you." Jesus cannot bear division. Get that deeply into your heart. And every time you think of anybody that differs from you, do make it a point to love him intensely before you talk about it.

But we read, "Jesus called them to Him, and saith unto them, 'Ye know that they who are accounted to rule over the Gentiles exercise lordship over them . . . but so shall it not be among you.'" Now listen! "But whosever will be great among you shall be your *minister* (or *servant*); and whoever of you will be chiefest shall be the servant of all." What teaching! But then comes: "For even the Son of man came not to be ministered unto, but to minister and to give His life a ransom for many," Now just let us look at this.

Look first at its connection with the preceding test that Christ proposes: Drink of My cup, and be baptized with My baptism." That is something spiritual *in their relation to Him.* But now He brings them down in the path of their consecration *to their relation to their fellowmen.* He says to them, in other words, "Not only like me must you give up your will in Gethsemane, and be baptized on Calvary, but remember, your consecration must be proved in your intercourse with each other every day, and by one consent you must all be servants." Is that what He expects? Yes it is. Humility is the test of discipleship, and humility is the only path to glory. God says, "He that humbleth himself shall be exalted. You cannot climb to the throne; but climb down, ever deeper down, and God will exalt you.

Let us take in this thought: Jesus came and "made himself of no reputation and took upon him the form of a servant." Have you said in your heart, "What divine beauty! My God taking the place of a *servant.*" Have you learnt it? If not, may you learn it tonight. The path of consecration is the path of humility. Jesus says that he who wants to be chief must be the bond slave of all. The least will be the chief.

You talk of the "primacy" in the church, of the "primate of all England." Christ says that the primate of all the churches is the very humblest. I wonder if we shall not have to be astonished in heaven at some poor, humble woman who will there take the first place. Just ask God, for Christ's sake, that the primate in the church may indeed be the very humblest in your circle. In your prayer meetings, just ask God to make him the very humblest, and then you will not get the spirit displayed by those disciples.

William Law gives some earnest advice about praying every day for humility as one of the most essential things we need, and he uses this strong expression—"Pray to be delivered from every vestige of pride as though you were in torment." Oh! Let us be afraid of pride, and let us live the life of humility. Jesus wants to bring us down.

"Even as the Son of man came not to be ministered unto, but to minister and to give His life," Oh, that wonderful word! *"Even as the Son of man."* that is our law, that is our rule to live by. How are we to live? He lived as a servant entirely to help others and make them happy. That is the work of the honest servant. Shall we not say to Jesus, "In thy name we take all God's people and become their servants, and ready we shall ever be to help them in any way."? Oh! May that spirit come upon us.

Ah! His death can do it. And you will need the power of His death to do it. For if we are to serve our brother—someone who worries us, and with whom there is friction—if we are to serve him every day and to keep the place of a humble slave, nothing less than the power of Christ's death will enable us to do it. We must live in the grave of Jesus. God bring us there and keep us there, even as the Son of man gave his life. And then you will be able to say increasingly, "Even as the Son I drink the cup, and even as the Son I am baptized into death, and even as the Son I give my life. I do not leave all the work to the missionary in the foreign field, but I say, 'Here is my life Lord; every hour is at Thy feet and at Thy disposal."

There we have the path to the higher life. It began with the prayer: "Nearness to Thee, likeness to Thee, power for Thee, O Jesus." Then came the words of Jesus to this effect: "You do not know what you are asking." Next is proposed the test of consecration: Can ye be baptized with the baptism? And then, after the disciples said they could, the loving answer came, the loving assurance, "Yes it shall be." Next followed that sad picture of the sin of contention. But praise God, even that has turned out for our good, for we have the blessed lesson coming out of it that we must learn to be the very least of all.

If therefore you want the steps in the path of consecration, they are these: Fellowship with Jesus; absolute and entire surrender to His death; fellowship with one another in love; a humility which gives itself to be the servant of all.

God make that the path of our consecration!

And now the very best part of my message I have yet to come to.

You will very naturally ask the question: The teaching of Christ, did it help much? Did it make Peter and James and John what they ought to be? I answer: Not a bit; they remained just as they were. And that teaches me the solemn lesson that Christ's teaching or convention teaching cannot cast out the devil.

The contention went on from this chapter down to the Last Supper. Pride and self-confidence were there, and in the hall of Caiaphas Peter denied his Lord. The teaching of Christ helped them very little, and yet—praise God—it did help them infinitely, for it prepared them by the consciousness of failure for something better. Did this ever come? It did come. At Pentecost everything was changed. Christ conquered sin and death and rose to heaven and sat on the right hand and received from the Father—yes, from His God and Father—a new gift, a new inflowing of the Holy Spirit. And by that Holy Spirit—although his teaching could not change them—came within them His own life, and then everything was changed.

Where did they get the power to "drink the cup?" Why was it that Peter was ready now for anything? Where did they get the power not to be afraid of imprisonment, to count it a joy to suffer and to give their lives even unto death? Where did they get it? At Pentecost the living Christ, the power of Gethsemane, the power of Calvary, the love that had died, entered into their hearts. Christ dwelt there, and from that day onward began a new life, a new era in the church of Christ.

And oh friends, I say that *that* is the best part of the message, for what I have to tell you in conclusion is: *all this is a divine possibility.* The previous speaker spoke of a plan of life in the case of a man who is half-hearted. I speak of a plan of life for a man who is whole-hearted. And I say to you, take the life-plan of Jesus and come tonight to Him and say, "Lord I will accept it; I can be baptized with Thy baptism."

Let us, ere we part, join in such an act of consecration.

***

Sermon 3: That God May Be All In All

"Then cometh the end, when He shall have delivered up the kingdom to God, even the Father; when He shall have put down all rule and all authority and power. For he must reign till He hath put all enemies under His feet. The last enemy that shall be destroyed is death. For He hath put all things under His feet. But when He saith, All things are put under Him, it is manifest that He is excepted, which did put all things under Him. And when all things shall be subdued unto Him, then shall the Son also Himself be subject unto Him that put all things under Him, that God may be all in all." (1 Corinthians 15:24–28)

*

These last words are my test. What a mystery there is in the context! We are accustomed to speak of the two great acts of humiliation on the part of the Lord Jesus—His descending from the throne and becoming man upon earth, a servant amongst men; and His descent through the cross into the grave—the depth of humiliation under the curse. But oh! What a mystery there is here—that there is a time coming in the everlasting glory when the Son of Man Himself will be subjected unto the Father, and shall give the kingdom into the Father's hands, and God shall be all in all. I cannot understand this; it passes knowledge. But I worship Christ in the glory of His subjection to the Father.

And here I learn one precious lesson, and that is what I want to point you to: that the whole aim of Christ's coming, and the whole aim of redemption, and the whole aim of Christ's work in our hearts is summed up in that one thought: *"That God may be all in all."* And if that is true, of what infinite consequence it is that you and I should take the thought as our life motto, and live it out. If we do not know that this is Christ's object, we never can understand what He expects of us and will work in us. But if we realize where it is all tending to—that everything must be subordinated to that—then we have a principal to rule our life, which was the very principle of the life of Christ.

Let us meditate a little while upon it, with the earnest prayer: "O God, we hope to be present on that wondrous day when Christ shall give up the kingdom and when Thou shalt be all in all." We hope to be there to see it and experience it, and to rejoice in it throughout eternity. O God, give us to know something of it here, this very night. Lord God, do take thy place, the place Thou hast a right to take, and reveal Thy glory, that every heart may be bowed in the dust and have but one song and one hope—*that God may be all in all.* O God, hear us, and may every heart be subjected to Thee tonight in full reality. Amen."

*

I said that this is what Jesus came into the world for. This is the object of redemption. This is what we must try to understand.

And I want to point you to two thoughts: First, see how Christ in his own life realized and worked this out—that God may be all in all. Second, see how we in our lives can realize it too.

If you look at the life of the Lord Jesus, then you see that there are five great steps in it. An old authority uses the very significant expression, "The Process of Jesus Christ." There is first His birth, then His life and His death and His resurrection and His ascension. In all these things you will see that God is all.

Look at His birth: He received it from God.

It was by an act of omnipotence that He was born of the Virgin Mary. It was from God that He had his mission, and He continually spoke of himself as being sent from God. Christ had his life from the Father, and He ever acknowledged it. And it is the first thing that a Christian must learn from Christ. We do not want to look at our conversion and say, "I did this" and "I did that,"—and perhaps to put in between—"God did that for me," but we want to take time in God's presence to say, "As truly as it was the work of Almighty God to give His Son here upon earth through the Virgin Mary, His life in human flesh, so truly and really has God given His life into my heart." We have our life from God.

Look at the next step: The life of Christ as Man to maintain.

He had to maintain it in the path God gave Him. How did He do it? He tells: "I can do nothing of Myself." He tells us that He did not speak one word till the Father had told Him. He just lived every moment of the day with this one thought: God is absolutely all, and I am nothing but a vessel in which God reveals His glory.

That was the life of Christ—entire, unbroken dependence upon God; and God really was in His life, every hour *all in all.* That was what Christ came to prove.

And notice that this was what man was created for: to be a vessel into which God could pour his wisdom and goodness and beauty and power. That is the nobility of the Christian. It is God that makes Seraphim and Cherubim flames of fire. The glory of God passes through them and they have nothing in themselves. They are just vessels prepared by God, come from God, that they might let God's glory shine through them.

And so it was with the Son. Sin came in, the terrible sin—first, of the fallen angels, and then of man. They exalted themselves against God, and would not receive the glory of God. And they fell into that "outer darkness," first the devils and then man. And Christ came to restore man, and so Christ lived among us, and day by day he just depended upon the Father for everything. Notice! He would not touch a bit of bread until the Father gave it to Him. He had the power, and He was very hungry, but He would not make a stone into bread—though He would have done it—until the Father said, "My Son eat this." Christ lived a life of absolute dependence upon God, waiting for God day and night. And that is the Man who is one day, in glory, to effect it that *God shall* be *all in all.*

Then next: He not only received His life from God, and lived it in dependence on God, but He gave it up to God.

He did it in obedience. What is obedience? Giving up my will to the will of another. When a soldier bows to his general, or a scholar to his teacher, he gives up his will. And my will is my life. He gives up himself to the rule and mastery and the power of another. And Christ did that. "*I came not to do mine own will. Lo, I come to do thy will.*" In Gethsemane He said, "*Not my will but Thine be done.*" Then he went further, and on the cross He carried out what had been settled in Gethsemane, and gave up His life to God. And He thereby taught us that the only thing that life is worth living for is *to give it back to God even unto death.*

If you take your life and spend it on yourself, even partly, you are abusing it, you are taking it away from its noblest use. Oh Christian, learn from Christ that the beauty of having life and will and body is that you can give it to God, and that then God will fill it with His glory. Yes, the Lord Jesus came and gave up his life unto the very death.

We have been talking about crucifixion and death more than once these days. Just let me say this in passing: We must not always look at crucifixion and death as necessary only from the side of sin. That is only half the truth—the negative side. But we must look at it from the other side—the side of the Lord Jesus. Why did He give up that life unto death, and what did He get by it? He gave up his earthly life, and God gave Him a heavenly life. He gave up the life of humiliation, and God gave Him a life of fellowship and glory.

Christian, do you want a life of fellowship with God and of glory and power and joy, even here upon earth? Remember then that there is but one way to secure it. Give your life up to

God. That is the one way. That is what Christ did. He gave up his life unto the very death, into the hands of God. Oh, do not you see that in the life of Christ, God was everything, God was all in all? Christ worked it out and proved most gloriously that God can be, and God must be, all in all.

Take the next step: He was raised again from the dead.

What does the resurrection mean? If you want to understand that, ask first, what does the cross mean? Jesus parted with his life and what does that say to us? He gave himself up into utter helplessness and impotence to wait upon God, to see what God would do. He said, "I cannot seize the heavenly life for myself. I wait till my father gives it to me." The grave was his humiliation. "My flesh shall rest in hope." There He waited until God the Father raised Him up in everlasting glory.

The time of Jesus in the grave was a very short time—only a portion of three days. But if there is one lesson we need to learn from Jesus, it is the lesson of the cross. Give up yourself in utter dependence upon God unto death. Lose everything and God will raise you up in glory. Christ could never have ascended to sit upon the throne, never could have accomplished His work of preparing the kingdom that He could give to the Father, if He had not begun by giving up Himself and let God do all. And it was even so too with His ascension to heaven and His entering into glory.

Well then, the five steps we have been considering are these: Christ had His life from God; He lived it in dependence upon God; He gave it up in death to God; He received it in the resurrection from God; and He ascended to God and was glorified in it with God forever.

And so, remember that the throne in heaven is not the throne of the Lamb of God alone. It is the throne of God and the Lamb. Jesus went to share the throne with the Father, and the Father was always the first and Jesus second. Even on the throne of heaven our glorified Lord Jesus honors the Father as Father, and honors God as God. It is a deep mystery, but it is the blessed subordination of the Son to the Father. Let us meditate until our souls get full of the thought and the blessed truth. The one thing that God must have He gets, even from His own Son: subordination, subjection. And it is because Christ sits in this spirit on the throne of Glory, that one day He can give up the kingdom to the Father.

Let us now take in this, which I said was my first great thought. The Lord Jesus came to remove the terrible curse that sin had wrought—the terrible ruin that had come by man's pride and self-exaltation. And He came to live out, during thirty-three years, *that God must be all in all.*

And let me ask in passing: Did God disappoint Him? I tell you, no. God lifted Him to the throne of the everlasting glory, and to equality on the throne with Himself because He had humbled Himself to honor His God. And if we want God to bless us, it is down in the place of dependence and humility that the blessing will be found.

But now we come to the second thought, and it is this: Are we called to live just as much as Christ did, *that God may be all in all?*

Is there any greater obligation on Christ to let God be all in all than on us? Most people think so, but the Bible does not. The obligation ought to be greater on us, for He is the Son of the Father, and God with God; but we are creatures of the dust. Oh, there can be no thought of our existence having been given for anything, but just for the blessed object that God may be all in all in us and to us. But have we understood that? And have we expected it? And have we sought for it? And have we ever learned to say with Christ, "It is worth giving up everything that God may have His place and be all in all?

But how can we attain to such a life? All our teaching about consecration will be moonshine unless it comes to this – that God must be *all*. What is the meaning of our talking about giving ourselves as a living sacrifice? It cannot be unless it is actually true that in our life God is *all*.

What is the reason of so much complaint of feebleness, of failure, of lost blessing, of walking in the dark? It is nothing but this: God does not get His place amongst us. I do not say that of the unsanctified, and the half-sanctified, but I say it of the best amongst us. God does not get His place. And I ask you tonight, O saints of God, to pray with your whole heart that God would take His place in the life of every one of us, and that the inconceivable majesty of God and His claim upon us be so revealed that we may sink as atoms in the dust and say, God be Thou all, and take all, and have all. God help us to do so.

Now what are the steps by which the soul can be brought, in some measure to live like Christ every day *so that God may be all in all?* My answer is, first of all: *Take time and trouble to give God His place.* Study your God, meditate more upon your God than you have done, and try to find out what is the place that God desires to take. And do not be content with the sought of vague conception: Yes, of course there is the throne in the heavens, and God is there. For remember, God is not only an outward Being, so to speak. There is a locality and a throne where the glory of God is specially revealed, but God has an inward being. He dwells even in Nature, and how much more in the heart of His redeemed ones and saints!

I want to get some conception of what is the place of God—and words can hardly tell. I can only say this: God is the fountain of all life. Every bit of life in the universe is the work of God. If you really give God His place, then you will get, oh, such a humbling conviction that there is nothing but what must come from God, that God fills all things. The Bible says He works all in all. And so you will begin to say: If God is everywhere and in everything, I ought always to see Him in Nature and in Providence and in everything. I ought always to be seeing my God. The believer can come to that when he sees God everywhere, and then he begins to give God his place. He cannot rise in the morning without giving God his place, and saying: Lord God Thou glorious Being, Thou art all in all.

And then He begins to say to his fellow believers: My brothers, I'm afraid that in our prayer meetings we do not let God take His place. We pray because we have a God to pray to, and we know something about God, but how little we in our souls realize the everlasting God! In our little prayer meetings the everlasting God of heaven is present, and if He gets his place, He will take charge of the prayer meetings, and He will give blessing and He will work by his mighty power.

Oh! Just think of it! Take our chairman for instance. He guides our meeting, he calls on one to pray and another to speak, and he tells us what to sing and give orders what is to be done. He has a little kingdom in this tent, and he manages it, and you are grateful for it. But God!—People do not allow Him to manage the Convention, or the prayer meeting. Do not we thank God for the chairman and the speaker, and for every earthly gift? But oh, that we might each learn to understand—in the Convention, in the church every Sunday, in the prayer meeting, in the closet—I must give time to let my God take His place.

Will God do it?

God is waiting to do it. *God longs to do it.* And then, not only in the closet and the prayer meeting, and the Convention and the church, but just as one of you takes the place of master and mistress in your house—as you sit at the head of the table, and you order the servant and you manage everything—so God is willing, in my heart and in yours, to take the place of Master and of God.

Brethren, have we given this glorious God the place He ought to have? Let us in our heart say 'No." And God forgive us if *we* have taken the place that Christ's redemption has given Him in us. Let us come tonight ere we part and say, "God shall have His place."

I might speak still further in the connection of the Church of Christ. Has God His place there? Alas, no! May God humble us and stir in us an unquenchable longing that God may be all in all. That is my first lesson: *Give God His place,* but take time and trouble to do it. Take heed and be quiet. The prophet says: "Be silent all flesh before the Lord." Let the flesh be kept down. Wait, and give God time to reveal himself.

Then the second point is: How am I in my life to attain this— that God may be all in all—and to work it out and prove it?

Accept God's will in everything. Where do I find God's will? I find God's will in His Word. I have often heard it reported that people have said, "I believe every word within these two covers has come from God." And I have sometimes heard it said, "I want to believe every promise between these two covers." But I have not often heard it said, "I accept every commandment within these two covers." But let me say it. If you like, write in the front page of your Bible what I once wrote in the front page of a young man's: "Every promise of God in this Book I desire to believe; every command of God in the book I desire to accept." That is one step in the way to let God be all in all. Give up your life to be the embodiment and expression and incarnation of the will of God.

Then further: Accept the will of God not only in the Bible, but especially in Providence.

I find thousands of Christians who have never learned that lesson. Do you know what that means? When Joseph's brethren sold him, he accepted God's hand in that, and it is written that when he went to Potiphar as a slave, "God was with him." He was not parted from God when he had to part from his home. I read of King Rehoboam, that when Shimei cursed him, he said in effect, "That is God." He saw God in that; he met God there in that cursing of Shimei. God was there all in all because God allowed it. When Judas came to kiss Christ and betray Him, and when the soldiers bound him, and when Peter denied Him, and when Caiaphas condemned Him, and when Pilate gave Him over, Christ saw God in everything. God was all in all; and so Christ could drink the cup, for He saw the hand of the Father holding it. Oh, let us learn, in every trial, in every trouble, great and little, to see God at once. Meet your God there, and let God be all in all.

There does not a hair of your head fall without the will of the Father. Meet the will of your Father in every trial, in the deepest and the heaviest; the Son of God walks there. Oh! Let God be all in all. And in the smallest trials—the servant who torments you, the child who hinders you, the friend who has hurt you by slight or neglect, the enemy who has reproached you, who has spoken evil of you and robbed you of your good name, the difficulty that worries you—Oh! Why don't you say, "God is all in all. It is my God who comes to me in every difficulty. I will meet Him and honor Him, and give myself to Him, and may He keep me!"

There are two great privileges of meeting God in a difficulty, and knowing Him. The first is that, even though the difficulty comes through my own fault, if I confess it, then I can say, "God has allowed me to come into this fault, to come into this difficulty in order to teach me a lesson. My God allowed me to come into it, and He must teach me to glorify Him in it."

If a father takes his child to a distant place to school, the child trusts his father to provide for him there. It is not willingly that the father sends the child away from under his eyes. And if God brings you into a difficulty by an act of your own, then you can count upon it that God will give you grace to be humble and patient and be perfected through the suffering and chastisement, that in everything He may take His place. You will be able to look to Him with double confidence when you say, "It is Thou who hast brought me here, and not man, and Thou alone canst take me out of it."

Oh! If you would only allow God to be all in all in every providence, what a blessed life you would be living! Nothing can separate you from the love of God in Christ Jesus. You have a wonderful place provided by His love. Oh! Learn to take this as the key out of every difficulty—*God is all in all.* And in prayer day by day, make it your earnest supplication that God may be all in all.

Then the third point. The first was: Give God His place; the second: Accept His will. The third is: Trust His almighty power.

Trust Him every day. I wish I could tell you rightly what, in this Convention, I see a glimpse of. And that is, that the whole of our Christian life every day is to be the work of God Himself. Paul speaks of it so often. *"It is God that worketh in you both to will and to do."* The will and the desire to obey— that is God's work in you, and that is only half of it. But He will work *"to do,"* as well as *"to will,"* if you will own Him practically in your life as *all in all.* In Hebrews we read: "The God of peace . . . make you perfect in every good work to do His will, working in you that which is well-pleasing in His sight, through Jesus Christ."

Here is my watch. Now, as surely as the watchmaker has made that watch, and worked at it and cut it and cleaned it and polished it and put in every little wheel and every little spring— just so the living God is actually and actively engaged in the work of perfecting your life every moment. God is willing to work in our meeting, from half-past six to half-past eight, every moment, and why doesn't He work more powerfully? Simply because you do not prove His power. You do not fully give Him His place. You do not wait upon Him to do it. Tell Him: "My God, here I am now. I give Thee the right place."

Now suppose a canvas could move about, and that when a painter came into his studio to paint an unfinished picture, it always removed to some other part of the room. Of course, then, the painter could not paint a single idea. But suppose the canvas began to say, "Oh, Painter, I will be still. Come and do thy work and paint thy beautiful picture. Then the painter would come and do it. And if you say to God, "Thou art the mighty Workman, the wondrous Workman. I am still. Here I am. I trust Thy power." Oh, believe it, God will then work wonders with you. God never works anything but wonders. That is His nature, even in what we call the laws of nature. Take the simplest thing: a blade of grass or a little worm or a flower. What wonders men of science tell us about them. And will not God work wonders in my heart and yours? He will. And why doesn't He do it more? Because we do not let Him. Oh, learn to give Him His place, to accept His will, and then to trust His mighty work.

In thy strength may I lie still,
The clay within the Potter's hand,
Moulded by thy gentle will,
Mightier that all command;
Shaped and moulded by Thee alone,
Now and ever more Thine own.

Is that true of You? God is willing to mold you as really as the potter molds his clay. He will do it. Let us believe it and trust His mighty power, and let us trust His power especially to do things above our conception, or above what we could ask or think.

Oh, that I could give every brother and sister before they leave Keswick a shake of the hand and tell them—but without it I tell them—*God is waiting to do for you more than you can even conceive.* I pray you, every yearning of your heart, every message that you have heard—of which you have said—I wish I had that. Every prayer you have sent up. Oh! Just believe that God is willing to work it all in you, and that He is waiting to do it; that in every difficulty, in every circumstance God is there to work in you. Trust Him and honor Him, and let Him be all in all.

And then, once again. If you would honor God, sacrifice everything for His kingdom and glory. If God is to be all in all, it must not be so much: I must be happy, and I must be holy, and I must have God's approval. No! The root principal of Christ's life was self-sacrifice unto God for man. That is what He came for, and it is a principle that every redeemed soul carries within Him as unquenchable. But alas! It can be smothered. But understand that your God longs to rule the world, and your Christ is upon the throne leading you on as His soldiers, and wanting to bless you with victory upon victory.

Have you given yourself up to God's glory? Alas, alas! The soldier upon earth says, "Anything for my king and country, anything when my general leads me on to victory. My home I leave and my comforts. I give my life. And are earthly kings to have such devotion, and you and I merely *talk* about the glory of God and His being all in all, when there is a call that we should help to prepare the kingdom for Christ to give up to the Father, and when Christ tells us He is waiting for our help and depending upon it?

Shall we not each say, God must be all in all; I will sacrifice everything for Him? May God help us tonight to make a consecration afresh of our whole being to the furtherance of Christ's kingdom. And whether it be in mission work far away, or in Christian work near at home, or whether it be that we do not know how to work, that we are poor weak worms—whatever it be—sacrifice everything and anything for the glory of your God. And if you do not know what to sacrifice, ask Him. Be honest, be earnest, be simple, be childlike and say, "Lord, every penny I have is Thine. If Thou needest it for Thy kingdom, I offer it to Thee.

Oh, in eternity, will a man grudge having made himself poor for the bringing about of that majestic spectacle, when the Son shall say, in a new sense, "It is finished," and give the kingdom to the Father, that God may be all in all? Do you hope to be there? Do you hope to have a share in the glory of that august scene? And are you willing tonight to say, "Anything I can do for that glory, Lord, here I am"? Give yourself up to Him.

And now the last thought, and that is: Wait on God.

I have been speaking and you thinking about God. That is one thing. But oh, to know God in His glory within our souls—that is another thing. I told you what you ought to do—that you ought to meditate and study, and to try to form a right conception of the place God should occupy in your life. But that is not enough. You must do something else. I said give yourselves up to the will of God, prove the power of God, and seek the glory of God throughout the earth. But the chief thing is, wait upon God.

And why must we do that? Because it is only God who can reveal Himself. Remember that when God came to Adam, or Noah or Abraham or Moses, it was God who came forth out of heaven and met them, and showed Himself in some form or other. That was under the old dispensation. And it depends today on the good pleasure of God to reveal Himself. Not an arbitrary good pleasure. No. It all depends upon whether He has found a heart hungering for Him. Oh, that God would give us that hunger and teach us to cry like David, "My soul thirsteth for God." Wait upon God. Make that in your closet a part of your life more and more systematically.

Do not be afraid if people say, "Do you want to make Quakers of us?" Let us remember that every portion of Christ's body has got a lesson for us. I do not think one of you will suffer if you learn the lesson, in your closet, of keeping silent before God—just with one prayer: "*Lord God, reveal Thyself in the depth of my heart.*" And though you do not expect a vision, though you do not get a manifestation—that is not what should be sought—it is that the soul should open itself to God and wait upon Him that He may come in. "Verily, thou art a God that hidest Thyself." You cannot see Him always, but He will come in and take possession of you—if you are ready for His incoming—and will reveal Himself and work mightily in you.

Wait upon God. In your prayer meetings, let that be the first thing. It is the mischief of our prayer in our closets and prayer meetings that we begin to pray at once, as if it was alright. "Oh yes," we say, "God will do it." And we do not take trouble to let our souls worship in holy awe and reverence and childlike trust. We do not take time to say, "Father, let it please Thee to come near and to meet me."

Some have said of the Convention—I think many—"Oh, if we could have more time for waiting upon God!" I think so too. I am a stranger. I do not want to be presumptuous, or to take unwarrantable liberty, but I do want to say that if next year it were so ordered by God that you could get that new hall, so that those people who wished it could go there to wait upon God in prayer—others being at liberty to go elsewhere to hear the speakers if they so desired—then I believe the result would be one of wonderful blessing.

The responsibility resting upon this body of believers is tremendous. We confess that many of us have got a secret which other Christians have not got, perhaps. We do not judge, but we confess that God has taught us something wonderful. Let us confess it boldly. But then, if that is true, we must get still nearer God, and have more of God in order to teach other Christians how they can find God. You cannot find God without waiting upon Him. "Wait, I say on the Lord."

Those are the steps by which we can come to have in our hearts and lives—*that God is all in all*—and the steps by which we can be prepared for taking part in that glorious company who shall be present on that magnificent occasion when Christ shall give up the kingdom to the Father—*that God may be all in all!*

*

Andrew Murray's 1895 Testimony

In Psalm 78:34 you have these words, "*When He slew them, then they sought Him.*"

*

When I was asked to give my testimony, I said I doubted whether it was desirable, and for this reason: We all know what helpfulness there is in the clear-cut testimony of a man who can say, "There I was: I knelt down and God helped me, and I entered the better life." I cannot give such a testimony; but I know what blessing it has often brought to me to read such a testimony for the strengthening of my faith. And yet, I got this answer from those who wished me to speak: "Perhaps there are many at Keswick to whom the testimony concerning a life of more struggle and difficulty will be helpful." I replied: "If it must be so, let me tell, for the glory of God, how He has led me.

A life on the lower stage

Some of you have heard how I have pressed upon you the two stages in the Christian life, and the step from one to the other. The first ten years of my spiritual life were spent manifestly on the lower stage. I was a minister, I may say, as zealous and as earnest and as happy in my work as anyone, as far as love of the work was concerned. Yet, all the time, there was burning in my heart—a dissatisfaction and restlessness inexpressible. What was the reason? I had never learned, with all my theology, that obedience was possible. My justification was as clear as noonday. I knew the hour in which I had received from God the joy of pardon.

I remember in my little room in Bloemfontein how I used to sit and think: "What is the matter? Here am I knowing that God has justified me in the blood of Christ, but I have no power for service." My thoughts, my words, my actions, my unfaithfulness—everything troubled me. Though all around thought me one of the most earnest of men, my life was one of dissatisfaction. I struggled and prayed as best I could.

Helped by the words from a missionary

One day, I was talking with a missionary. I do not think he knew much of the power of sanctification himself—he would have admitted it. When we were talking and he saw my earnestness, he said, "Brother, remember that when God puts a desire into your heart, He will fulfill it." That helped me; I thought of it a hundred times. I want to say the same to you who are plunging about and struggling in the quagmire of helplessness and doubt. The desire that God puts in your heart, He will fulfill.

Helped by the book: *Parables from Nature*

I was greatly helped about this time by reading a book called *Parables from Nature*. One of these parables represents the thought that after the creation of the earth, a number of crickets met on a certain day. One of them began saying, "Oh I feel so happy. For a time I was creeping about looking for a place to stay, but I could not find the place that suited me. At last I got in behind the bark of an old tree, and it seemed as though that place was just fitted for me; I felt so comfortable there."

Another said, "I was there for a time, but it did not fit me." (That was a grass cricket.) "But at last I got on to a high stalk of grass, and as I clung there and swung there in the wind and in the air, I felt that that was the place made for me."

Then a third cricket said, "Well, I have tried the bark of the old tree, and I have tried the grass, but God has made no place for me, and I feel unhappy." Then the old mother cricket said, "My child, do not speak that way. Your creator never made anyone without preparing a place for him. Wait, and you will find it in due time."

Sometime after, these same crickets met together again, and got to talking. The old mother said, "Now my child, what say you?" The cricket replied, "Yes, what you said is true. You know those strange people who have come here. They built a house, and in their house they had a fire; and you know, when I got into the corner of the hearth near the fire, I felt so warm, and I knew that that was the place God made for me."

That little parable helped me wonderfully, and I pass it on to you. If any are saying that God has not got a place for them, let them trust God and wait, and He will help you, and show you what is your place.

You know God led Israel forty years in the wilderness; and that was my wilderness time. I was serving Him very heartily, yet it was dark very often, and the great burden on my heart was, "I am sinning against the God that loves me."

Called to Worcester

So the Lord led me till, in his great mercy, I had been eleven or twelve years in Bloemfontein. Then He brought me to another congregation in Worcester, about the time when God's Holy Spirit was being poured out in America, Scotland and Ireland. In 1860, when I had been six months in the congregation, God poured out His Spirit there in connection with my preaching, especially as I was moving about in the country, and a very unspeakable blessing came to me. The first Dutch edition of my book *Abide in Christ* was written at that time.

I would like you to understand that a minister or Christian author may often be led to say more that he has experienced. I had not then experienced all that I wrote of; I cannot say that I experience it all perfectly even now. But if we are honest in seeking to trust God in all circumstances, and always to receive the truth, He will make it live in our hearts. But let me warn you, Convention Christians, not to seek too much satisfaction in your own thoughts or the thoughts of others. The deepest and most beautiful thoughts cannot feed the soul unless you go to God and let Him give you reality and faith.

Always seeking and always getting

Well, God helped me, and for seven or eight years I went on, always inquiring and seeking, and always getting. What we want is to trust God more. He helped me to trust Him in the dark and in the light. Then came, about 1870, the great Holiness Movement. The letters that appeared in *The Revival*—now *The Christian*—touched my heart; and I was in close fellowship with what took place at Oxford and Brighton, and it all helped me.

Perhaps, if I were to talk of consecration, I might tell you of an evening there in my own study in Cape Town. Yet, I cannot say that that was my deliverance, for I was still struggling. I would say that what we need is complete obedience. Let us not be like Saul, who, after he was anointed, failed in the case of Agag [King of Amalek] to accept God's judgment against sin to the very utmost.

Later my mind became much exercised about the baptism of the Holy Spirit, and I gave myself to God as perfectly as I could to receive the baptism of the Spirit. Yet there was failure; God forgive it. It was somehow as if I could not get what I wanted. Through all these stumblings, God led me without any very special experience that I can point to; but as I look back, I do believe now that He was giving me more and more of His blessed Spirit, had I but known it better.

Not a marked experience, but what God has given me now

I can help you more, perhaps, by speaking, not of any marked experience, but by telling very simply what I think God has given me now, in contrast to the first ten years of my Christian life.

In the first place, I have learned to place myself before God every day as a vessel to be filled with His Holy Spirit. He has filled me with the blessed assurance that He, as the everlasting God, has guaranteed His own work in me. If there is one lesson I am learning day by day, it is this: It is God who worketh all and in all. Oh, that I could help any brother or sister to realize this!

I will tell you where you fail. You have never yet heartily believed that He is working out your salvation. You believe that if a painter undertakes a picture, he must look to every shade of color and every touch upon the canvas. You believe that if a workman makes a table or bench, he knows how to do his work. But you do not believe that the everlasting God is working out the image of His Son in you, as any sister here is doing a piece of ornamental or fancy work, following out the pattern in every detail. Just think, "Can God not work out in me the purpose of His love?" If that piece of work is to be perfect, every stich must be in its place. And remember that not one minute of your life should be without God.

We do not believe that. We want God to come in at times—say, in the morning; then we are to live two or three hours, and He can come in again. No! God must be *every moment the worker of your soul.*

I may abide in His presence unceasingly

I was once preaching, and a lady came to talk with me. She was a very pious woman, and I asked her, "How are you going on?" Her answer was, "Oh, just the way it is always; sometimes light and sometimes dark." "My dear sister, where is that in the Bible?" She said, "We have day and night in nature; and just so it is in our souls." "No, no; in the Bible we read, '*Your sun shall no more go down.*'"

Let me believe that I am God's child, and that the Father in Christ, through the Holy Ghost, has set His love upon me and I may abide in His presence—not frequently, but unceasingly. The veil has been rent; the Holist of All has been opened. By the grace of my God, I have there to take up by abode; and there my God is going to teach me what I never could learn while I dwelt outside. My home is always the abiding love of my Father in Heaven.

You will ask me, "Are you satisfied? Have you got all you want?" God forbid! With the deepest feeling of my soul, I can say I am satisfied with Jesus now; but there is also the consciousness of how much fuller the revelation can be of the exceeding abundance of His grace. Let us never hesitate to say, "This is only the beginning." When we are brought into the Holist of All, we are only beginning to take our right position with the Father.

May He teach us our own nothingness and transform us into the likeness of His Son, and help us to go out and be a blessing to our fellow-men. Let us trust Him and praise Him in the midst of a consciousness of our own utter unworthiness, and in the midst of a consciousness of failure and a remaining tendency to sin. Notwithstanding this, let us believe that our God loves to dwell in us; and let us hope without ceasing in His still more abundant grace.

*

Andrew Murray at Exeter Hall

Exeter Hall London

Foreword

When Andrew Murray first arrived in England on the first leg of his preaching tour in 1895, leaders in the Christian community in London arranged a welcome breakfast for him at Exeter Hall. After his six-month preaching tour of England, Holland and the USA, he returned to London. But now he was a celebrated preacher whose fame preceded him. His sermons were of such note that they were even reported in the British Weekly of 29 November. An excerpt from their article reads:

> *Everywhere the people have gathered in crowds to hear him. His discourses are delivered without the use of manuscript or notes. . . . The two great meetings at Exeter Hall were the most successful of the series. They were announced to begin at seven, but after half-past six, it was difficult to get a seat. The interval of waiting was spent in the singing of hymns.*

The talks recorded in this little book were the last he gave at Exeter Hall. But unlike the sermons delivered in the main auditorium, where thousands gathered to hear him, these were given in a smaller meeting room to the same group of leaders and full-time Christian workers who had welcomed him to London four months before.

Shortly after Andrew Murray delivered them, they were published as part of the 'Upward Life Series' under the title *Eagle Wings* in 1896.

***

Three sermons on prayer given

at

Exeter Hall

Sermon 1: That They All May Be One

Neither pray I for these alone, but for them also which shall believe on me through their word; that they all may be one; as thou, Father, art in me, and I in thee, that they also may be one in us: that the world may believe that thou hast sent me. And the glory which thou gavest me I have given them; that they may be one, even as we are one: I in them, and thou in me, that they may be made perfect in one; and that the world may know that thou hast sent me, and hast loved them, as thou hast loved me. (John 17: 20-23)

*

The words from which I wish to speak to you are found in John 17. We shall take from **verse 20** the words: "*I pray.*" We shall take from verse 21: "*That they all may be one; as thou, Father, art in me, and I in thee, that they also may be one in us: that the world may believe that thou hast sent me.*" And from verse 22: "*And the glory which thou gavest me I have given them.*"

Note that the 20th verse says, "*I pray* (or, I ask Thee)." The 22nd verse says, "*And the glory which thou* gavest me I have given them"—with the same aim: "that they may be one, even as we are one." The 23rd verse: "*I in them, and thou in me, that they*

may be made perfect in one; and that the world may know that
thou hast sent me, and hast loved them, as thou hast loved me."

The desire for overflowing love

If I judge aright as to what fills your hearts this morning, then I think I would express it this way: There is a deep consciousness that there is not among the people of God that overflowing love that there should be. There is the desire to see this changed, and there is the secret faith that if God chooses He is able to change us.

But there is more. Your coming here is, I trust, a testimony to the positive expectation that if we ask Him, He will pour out more love among His people. We want this morning to make confession of this want of love. We want to cry to God for an increase of love.

I need not remind you of what the proofs are that love is so often lacking. I will not speak of the divisions among the churches. I will not speak of the way in which Christians speak of each other. I will not speak of the coldness often existing between Christians who spend years together in the same church and eat the same bread at the Lord's Supper. I will not speak of how the most precious truths and promises of God unconsciously become walls of separation. You all know. You all deplore that there is not that love whereby the world is compelled to say, "God has loved them, and has poured His love into their hearts."

And now, if we are to make confession, and if we are to be encouraged to pray, to hope, and to expect deliverance, nothing is better than that we should turn for a few minutes to

God's blessed Word—the words of our great High Priest in His last prayer. You know them well. He prayed, "*Father, . . . I pray . . . that they all may be one.*" It was God who was to do it. Then He added wonderful words to the effect: "Father, between Thee and Me there has never been anything but love, and I want that to be among my people, that they may be one, even as We are One."

And then he says, in words similar to these: "Father, it will be such a wonderful thing when selfish, proud men learn to love as the Father and the Son of God love. Then the world will be compelled to say, 'That is more than human love; that is a love that comes from Heaven.'"

Then Christ goes on to say, in effect, "Father, it is for this that I have given them the glory that Thou gavest Me, and have made them partakers of the Divine nature, and of all that Thou hast. And, Father, on that account, I pray for them. I have given them the glory that thou gavest Me; and now, Father, watch over that glory that they may be one as We are, and that they may be made perfect in one, that the world may believe that thou hast sent me, and hast loved them as Thou hast loved Me." What a prayer!

Now, what are the thoughts that this prayer on the oneness of God's people suggest to us?

First: The oneness among God's people is to be the reflection of the life of God in Heaven.

Just think of that! Heaven is the place where the glory of God is perfectly manifested. Earth is the place where the reflection of the glory is to be seen. Yonder in the heavens, the sun burns in all its brightness, heat, and glory. Here on earth, miles and miles away, is the place where the light is shining. And yonder in Heaven is the glory of God's love; but here on earth it is a beautiful, reflected light. And what is that light to be? We are to love one another and be one, just as the Father and the Son are one.

Oh, beloved, have we really taken it in? Think of the love of the Father to the Son. What is it? The Father gave all that he had to the Son. That is His love, and that is to be my love to you and your love to me. It is to be nothing less, for that is holiness, that is perfection, and that is happiness. God wants you holy, perfect, happy, and like himself. That is love! God gave all He had to His beloved Son.

And what was the love of the Son to the Father? He gave all back. When He had taken a human body, when he had come here in the flesh, He gave all. He gave His obedience, He gave his life, and gave His all to the Father. That was love! He loved the Father in eternity, and sought nothing for himself. He loved the Father amid temptation and sufferings on the earth.

And now, that love of the Father to the Son, and that love of the Son to the Father, is to be the measure of our love to each other, children of God. I do not ask, "Have you attained that?" But I may ask, "Have you aimed at that? And has it been your study and heart-cry: 'O my God! Help me to love as You love and as Jesus loves'"? Yes, the Lord Jesus said so, and more than once. He said, "A new commandment I give unto you, that ye love one another as I have loved you" (John 13: 34). He came with that love, and He was prepared by the Holy Spirit to implant it in the hearts of the disciples, who had been unloving.

"Love one another as I have loved you." Christ gave us that command. Have we understood it? It is something necessary to talk about the want of love in the Church of Christ. And it is sometimes necessary to forget it, and to come to my own heart and ask, "How is it with my love to the brethren?"

That is our first thought: The oneness of God's people is to be the reflection of the very life of God in Heaven.

Then next: That oneness is to be the manifestation of the mighty power of God.

It is a thing God has to do. The Lord Jesus Christ did not say, "Father they are one." He said, *"I pray . . . that they all may be one."* God was to do it. Just as Christ asked God to glorify Him in Heaven (in the beginning of the prayer), so here (at the end), He asks the Father, in effect, "Do this too, and grant that they may be one, even as we are." Beloved, God has to do it.

And there comes the great fault, the great reason why there is so little love. We do not count upon God to do it. God puts a seed, a principle, a power of divine love and a new will into the heart of every child of His who is born of the Holy Spirit. And for this reason every child of God is by his very nature inclined to love God's children. But after a time, there comes trial, and it becomes difficult to love. The Christian often begins to try, in the power that is in him, to love as he should, but fails. Afterwards, he gives way to despair. and begins with his little love to do his very best, but he can never love like the Bible wants him to.

Ah! He misunderstood God's plan. God's plan is this: *"It is God which worketh in you both to will and to do"* (Philippians 2: 13).

When He has first worked *to will,* you are still impotent. But He wants you to come and claim the power of the Holy Spirit to enable you *to do.*

I have spoken much and long about the Holy Spirit, but I am coming to the conviction—which I may say grows deeper every day—that we know very little of what the Holy Spirit can do. I believe that the word of St. Paul that says, "*The love of God shed abroad in our hearts by the Holy Spirit*" (Romans 5: 5) means: that just as Paul was filled with the love of God; and just as Paul could say, "*The love of Christ constraineth me*;" and just as Paul lived incessantly, day and night, praying for his people; and just as Paul poured out his love with all the tenderness of a mother or a nurse—as he tells us himself—so God's Holy Spirit can fill the heart and life to the extent that love will be to us as natural as the love of a mother towards her child.

The Lord Jesus Christ, our High Priest, cried to His Father to make us one. But we try in our own strength to love, and fail, instead of coming utterly impotent and helpless to claim a new blessing—to claim that the Holy Spirit should fill us and shed abroad, through our whole being, the almighty love of God.

It is good that we have come together today. My heart is glad to see God's children longing to hear about love. But everything will be like "the morning cloud and the early dew" (Hosea 6: 4), and our aim and purpose to love will vanish unless God gives His Holy Spirit in power into our hearts.

Do let every heart bow before God this morning. We are going to undertake the work of love by giving up ourselves to intercession and thinking of what God wants us to do in intercession. But if we are really to have the spirit of intercession, we must have the love of our Emmanuel, the Lamb of God. Come this morning! Ask God to give you His almighty love in a measure and in a way and in a power you have never understood. Even now, He can set your heart upon it. God can make your heart a vessel for that love. He will delight to do it.

Then comes the next thought: Love comes in answer to prayer.

I have spoken about the great power of God doing it, but I now want to point out that Christ prayed for it. He prayed: "*that they all may be one*." Oh! That our hearts may—just for a moment—look up and see our Lord Jesus, to hear by the Holy Spirit that prayer which goes up—not in words—but in His holy presence and power: "*Father, . . . that they all may be one*"! He prays for them without ceasing. He lives to pray for them.

And what does this call us to? To praying with Him in His name, and in His Spirit, and with great faith in the fellowship of His intercession. When we start praying more for an outpouring of love in our hearts and in the hearts of God's children around us, a change in the Church will come.

Allow me here, my beloved friends, to come at once to what has been on my heart: That God's children ought every day of their lives to pray for all believers. Paul did not tell Christians in his Epistles to pray for the heathen, the Jews, or the unconverted, but he always told them to pray for "all saints." They are the members of our body. They are our brothers and sisters. And until we cry every day to God for the body of the Church in our daily devotions as much as we cry to Him for our own souls, I do not believe that a great revival of love will come. But

I think God will pour it into the hearts of His children as the beginning and earnest of what He is going to do.

Do pray for Christians every day of your lives. I do not want you to give up any union you may have joined to pray at certain times for specific circles of believers, but I want you to feel that it ought to be a continuous part of the spiritual life. Just as close as my relationship is to Christ, so is my relationship to my fellow Christians. And just as dependent as I am upon Christ in some things, so I am dependent for others on the fellowship of the saints. Every thought of Christ ought to be linked with the thought of His people, His body, the Church. By prayer it will come.

Before we part this morning, may God give us the very spirit of prayer in our hearts in such a way that we shall continually cry: "O God, make us one as You and Your Son are One!" The cry will lead us to feel our own impotence as well as the loneliness and feebleness of our lives.

Remember what Paul said to the Thessalonians, "*Ye yourselves are taught of God to love one another. And indeed ye do it*" (1 Thessalonians 4: 9-10). And yet further on in verse 10 he wrote beseeching them "That ye increase more and more." There is increase in love when the Holy Spirit touches the heart, for then love will flow in a stream, and it will be one of those streams of which Jesus spoke when he said, "*He that believeth in me, out of him will flow rivers of living water*" (John 7: 38). This living water is to impart what the fountain has got, and thereby make all around green and fresh. This stream of love will impart of itself to bless others. We must pray that this oneness may be made manifest.

But another thought: The manifestation of this oneness upon earth is to be a proof to the world that God sent Christ, and that God has loved us.

Just think of that! How important it is! You know Christ Jesus himself said, *"By this shall all men know that ye are my disciples (a heavenly people), if ye have love one to another"* (John 13: 35). That is to be the heavenly mark, and He says it twice in our text.

First of all He says, *"I pray . . . that they all may be one, . . . that the world may believe that thou hast sent me"* (John 17: 15, 21). You know that Christ was amongst them in the world, and they would not believe it. And what was to bring conviction? *Love.* That is what Christ said. Not preaching, but *love.* Preaching is needed—praise God for what it does!—but love will do more.

In the next two verses He says, "And the glory which thou gavest me I have given them; that they may be one, even as we are one . . . that the world may know that thou has sent me, and has loved them, as thou hast loved me." God loved Christ with a wonderful love. And God loves His people with the same love; and the love with which God loves Christ became a love that He poured out upon us, even unto the blood of Calvary. And the love with which God and Christ love us will be within us a power that will pour itself out, in the first place, for the brethren; and by it the world will be convinced.

People speak of the evidence of Christianity, and books have been written on the evidences of Christianity, and they are not without their value, though I do not know that they have turned many from darkness to light. But Christ says it is love that will compel the world to say, "These men have got something from Heaven. These men are living a superhuman life. Just look at the way in which they love each other!"

Dear friends, has the world around us, or any part of it, been convinced, been convicted, and brought to acknowledge: "God sent Christ, and God loves that man just as He loves Christ? I can see it, for there is something in him I cannot find upon earth"? Praise God! There have been such cases. There are believers of whom others have felt that they have got something that is not on earth. But how little that is the case!

And why should it not be the case with each one of us? It is just this: One thing is needed. We must wait upon God in prayer. Let me point out to you one text to impress that thought upon you. In 1 Thessalonians 3:12, what do you read? "*And the Lord make you to increase and abound in love one toward another.*" Now note that just as Christ prayed to the Father, so Paul prayed: "*The Lord make you to increase and abound in love.*" And he uses the same expression in 1 Thessalonians 4:9-10: "*As touching brotherly love ye need not that I write unto you: for ye yourselves are taught of God to love one another. And indeed ye do it toward all the brethren which are in Macedonia: but we beseech you brethren that ye increase more and more.*" Christ said, in effect, "Love one another as I have loved you" (John 15: 12). And Paul said the same: "*The Lord make you to . . . abound in love, even as we do toward you*" (1 Thessalonians 3: 12).

I now press upon you to notice those words which follow in 1 Thessalonians 3:13: "***To the end*** *He may stablish your hearts unblameable in holiness before God.*" Did you ever notice that phrase: *To the end*? How is God going to make me holy and establish my heart unblameable in holiness? By filling me with love. *Love* is the fulfillment of the whole law and the perfection of the life of God and of Christ. And when God makes us to increase in love and to abound in love toward one another, then self sinks away, and the love of God takes possession, and the love and holiness of God can grow and prosper and rule within us.

Let us take that prayer for ourselves today: "The Lord make **us** to increase and abound in love one toward another . . . to the end He may establish **our** hearts unblameable in holiness before God."

In conclusion: What is needed if in answer to prayer this love of God is to come and take possession of our souls?

The heart must be utterly and absolutely given up to God to love. May God this day enable us to see how little there has been of the real heavenly love within us. May God enable us to make confession of it.

How much self has limited our love to people that we agree with, and to people that we like, and to people that think just as we do! How much our love has been limited within our own circle, and how little it has gone out as love to the unworthy, to those who differ from us, to those who do not love us! Ah, brethren! Have you studiously tried to love every man from whom you feel you would rather be separate? Have you made it a study to pray: "Lord here is one in whom my love can triumph, in whom Your love can triumph; I want to love him as a brother"? May God give us the spirit of humility to confess how little we have of divine love.

Just when we try, at times, we have the proof of how the spirit of love has not yet triumphed within us. But praise God! The Father on whom Christ called, to whom Paul prayed, to whom we come to pray today—the Father in Heaven—wants to give His Holy spirit of love to us. Even before we make intercession for an outpouring of the spirit of love upon the Church, we want to ask for an outpouring of the Spirit into our own hearts. We want to say, "Lord God, empty our hearts of self. We desire to confess and give up everything that is selfish. We desire to study and aim at this one thing: to live on earth towards every brother as God and Christ live together in Heaven.

You might say, "But God and Christ see nothing but what is lovely in each other. How can they, therefore, do otherwise than love each other? By contrast, my brother tempts me so. There is so much in him that is hard and unlovable. Ah, yes! It was for that that the Son of God came to earth to prove that the love of God in Heaven could stand the trials of life—every enmity, every shame, every suffering—and live through it all. And it is your high privilege to have your heart filled with the heavenly love of Christ Jesus, and to carry it through life. And it is your high privilege to begin to prove that you love your brother.

You might find it difficult to love the unlovely, and yet you sometimes tell me, "I find it easier to love the ungodly that to love my very brother." Oh! What a proof of your blindness! Praise God for love to the ungodly. But that brother of yours—redeemed with the blood of Christ, a member of one body in one Spirit with you through Christ Jesus—what a thought that you cannot love that brother!

Oh! Come today and let us confess our sin, our utter impotence. Let us look up in faith and claim the mighty power of God's Spirit. Let us claim in faith the promise: "The love of God is shed abroad in our hearts by the Holy Spirit who is given unto us."

Then, when we have yielded ourselves up to God, let us begin to plead and pray for God's Church around us, for every professing child of God in London and in England. But let us begin to pray a prayer that shall never cease: "Lord, visit Your saints." Oh, that God may write this upon our hearts!

Who are willing to give themselves up to this glorious work of prayer for the saints of God and for a revelation of God's love in Christ's body? Let their hearts say to God, "Lord, here I am." That will help you get a blessing of love for yourself. But if you want love that is going to plead for the body of Christ, then you must do two things: Go and confess to God your lack of love and say, "Lord God, I want to have that love, so that from this day forwards I may daily pray for all believers." God will give it. The great intercession of Christ secures it.

***

Sermon 2: The Secret of Effectual Prayer

Likewise the Spirit also helpeth our infirmities: for we know not what we should pray for as we ought: but the Spirit itself maketh intercession for us with groanings which cannot be uttered. And he that searcheth the hearts knoweth what is the mind of the Spirit, because he maketh intercession for the saints according to the will of God. (Romans 8: 26-27)

*

In these words we have the secret of effectual prayer.

Since the morning meeting, someone complained to me: "I feel so little love for prayer and power for prayer." *Here* is the power for prayer: the *Holy Spirit*.

So many complain that they do not feel strong stirrings of desire to intercede for others. *Here* is the secret power: "*The Spirit also helpeth our infirmities.*" Would God that we could learn that precious lesson!

What are the thoughts suggested to us here?

The first thought is this: If you want to discover the secret of effectual prayer, you must begin with a sense of your own ignorance.

When does the Holy Spirit come? When a man says, "I cannot pray." But when a man says, "I can pray," there is no room for the Spirit to work in full power. Alas! How often we think it is easy to pray. We think, "I learnt it from my mother; I learnt it from my minister; I learnt it when I was converted; I learnt it from written prayers. And so, though we think we know how to pray, there may be at the back—alas!—a deep ignorance of praying for what God wants us to pray for. We may be praying very earnestly for what *we* think, and yet not allow God's Spirit to teach us what *God* thinks.

Therefore, if you want to pray in power, begin with these words: "*The Spirit also helpeth* (is given to help) *our infirmities.*" Just as Paul said, "*When I am weak then I am strong . . . that the power of Christ may rest upon me*" (2 Corinthians 12:10,9, so it is here. When I feel my infirmities in prayer, then the Holy Spirit will help me. It is when I learn to say and live in the experience and consciousness: "I know not what to pray for as I ought," that I have a claim upon the promise of the Holy Spirit's help.

Have you ever studied the blessedness of ignorance? Oh, the divine blessedness of ignorance! "God hath chosen the foolish things of the world" (1 Corinthians 1:27). That is no mere idea; it is a reality. Abraham went out not knowing where he was to go, but he had God for his Guide. So through the whole of God's Word you will find that it continually comes up that when a man is ignorant and at his wit's end, and says, "I know not what to do," God comes in to take charge.

Remember the Holy Spirit cannot come to you in prayer as the Spirit of prayer and intercession, unless this double thought is deep in your life: *"I do not know rightly what to pray for,* and *I do not know how to pray as I ought."* There are so many Christians who think this thought to be a terrible burden and a great sorrow. But I tell you, it is your highest privilege if you use it correctly, by saying, "Lord, I cannot pray, but let your blessed Spirit pray with me."

In this great work of intercession that we are going to be engaged in, to talk about, and to undertake—not only for today, but for the future—let us remember that our ignorance will be the secret of success if we use it aright. "I know what to pray for," you say. "Yes, I can read my Bible, and know the needs of my heart and the needs of the world around me. Oh yes, I need to pray for London, for God's Church and for the heathen." Oh! How much of that praying is the work of the mind, the work of the flesh, the work of man! Do not be afraid of letting the following words take hold of you: *"We know not what to pray for as we ought."* That is the first step.

What is the next? That we begin to learn that the Holy Spirit has been given from Heaven into our hearts to teach us to pray.

"The Spirit . . . helpeth our infirmities." Have you realized that God not only answers prayer, but that God, dwelling within us by the Holy Spirit, inspires prayer? If that is true, what would be the effect of my believing fully?

First of all, it would be an abasement before God, and a humiliation and a dependence expressed in this way: "O God, may I not in the power of the flesh and the thought of my mind hinder the blessed Spirit. And then there would come a deep subjection and surrender to the Spirit, and the deep consciousness: "I must give up my life for Him to live in me, or He cannot pray in me." We should then get rid of that terrible thought that we can at times get the Holy Spirit to come and do something for us. We should understand that He must be the very Spirit of our life. He must have entire possession.

Have you ever learnt this solemn, blessed lesson: "The Holy Spirit and I are linked together in prayer, and God wants the Holy Spirit, dwelling in the body of Christ, to teach each individual of that body to pray aright in the power of faith."? Have you ever learnt that lesson? If not, may God open it up to you this afternoon.

And when the question comes, "What is needed that I may get the Spirit?" The answer will be this: "As a surrendered soul, I am entirely at His disposal. He is not a person outside of me. He comes in to be my very life. And unless I give myself up to Him, how can He do His blessed work and fully teach me how to pray?"

That brings us to a very solemn point in this meeting. Some days ago, someone was telling me of a person that she wanted to bring with her, and she said, "I am afraid she is not a surrendered soul." And, in another case, somebody said of one who was going to come, "Ah, that is one who is still undecided—halfway between Christ and the World."

Now if there are souls here—children of God who are not utterly surrendered to Him—I plead with you before I go further. By the mercy of God, think about it. The Holy Spirit cannot dwell in a worldly heart. The Holy Spirit cannot do His blessed work in a life that is not given up to Him. Come today, if you have any desire for the full blessing, and say, "If God has given His Holy Spirit to pray in me, I will give my whole heart to Him. If you have never yet in faith claimed the promise of the full indwelling of the Holy Spirit, come today and claim it.

Your God offers you the Holy Spirit to pray in you, and how can He do it if you grieve Him, if you distrust Him, and if, by unbelief, you dishonor Him? Oh! I want to invite all God's children here to become intercessors, but we cannot do it unless we all join in saying: "O God, discover in us everything in which the Holy Spirit has not complete possession. We desire to give it up and to be filled with your Spirit."

I feel more and more deeply, every time I address meetings, that you may have an earnest Christian—a godly man or woman—whose life may be far below what God is able to make it, if he or she would only wait for the Holy Spirit to get possession. Believers, I want to call you to be intercessors. I want to plead with you by the needs of London—with its five million people; by the needs of heathenism—with its hundreds of millions; and by the needs of the Church of Christ—alas! alas!—with its multitudes of nominal professors and half-hearted Christians. Will you not be intercessors? Will you not give up yourselves to walk in the footsteps of Christ and to become fountains of blessing to this weary world? Oh! Come and let the Holy Spirit have you entirely today, and then He will teach you how to pray.

A third thought: We must understand the way in which the Holy Spirit will pray.

And what way is that? "The Spirit also helpeth our infirmities: for we know not what we should pray for as we ought: but the Spirit itself maketh intercession for us with groanings which cannot be uttered" (Romans 8: 26).

What are these groanings? Prayers too deep for words. That is what we want. When the words can rise into a prayer so fluently and so easily—alas!—the depth of the heart is often not stirred.

But what does the Holy Spirit want to do? How often we see it in our blessed Lord Jesus! Do we not read that He once said, "*I have a baptism to be baptized with; and how am I straightened till it be accomplished!*" (Luke 12:50). You remember again that he said, "*And what shall I say? Father save me from this hour*" (John 12:27). He did not know at the moment what he should say. And yet again, you know how in Gethsemane He wrestled and wrestled, and yet had but few words with which to utter the agony of His heart.

Oh, brethren! When the Holy Spirit comes within us as the fire of God's love for souls, and we begin to think of the state of Christ's body—of our brethren in the Church of Christ, of our own want of love and tenderness and gentleness, of the feebleness that marks God's people, of the way the world loves to scorn our puny efforts, and of the millions who are going down to misery—surely there will come to us (if God's Spirit only got possession of us) a burden, a sorrow, an intensity, and a desire too deep for words. Then is the time when the Holy Spirit prays in us "with groanings that cannot be uttered."

We read of creation "groaning." There is a moan throughout creation, and a longing for redemption. The animals do not speak it out in words, but throughout creation there is a groan. Even so, the deeper God's child is led into the fellowship of Christ and love for souls, the deeper and the truer his sympathy is with the perishing. Then there will come times when he can only sit still before God, and say, "Lord, what is to come of it? Oh! Teach me what I may pray. And while he feels that he cannot pray, God has heard in that heart a better prayer than one that flows so smoothly and quickly from the lips.

Many a one thinks that when they have been in their closet and prayer has flowed easily, that they have prayed well. And they think, at other times, when prayer has not flowed easily, that they have not prayed well. And yet, if the silent prayer were mingled with true faith plus a waiting upon God and a deep, burning desire, it was a sweeter incense to the Father than a prayer that came in words.

Oh! It is a solemn thing for a worm of the dust to get linked to the Holy Spirit of God. You cannot wonder that the Holy Spirit of God will sometimes come with wrestlings and groanings that cannot be uttered. But the privilege and blessedness are unspeakable. Oh! Let us yield ourselves to Him.

And then comes the last thought in my text: The believer must know how the answer will come.

How can it come when I sit there sad and burdened with a burden I cannot speak out? Listen! "He that searcheth the hearts knoweth what is the mind of the Spirit, because he maketh intercession for the saints according to the will of God" (Romans 8: 27). Oh, think of that! God, the Heart-searcher, is needed to find out the meaning of a prayer. You think you know it, but it needs God in Heaven, who searches the hearts, to measure the real value of a prayer. We deceive ourselves. We have sometimes felt: "Oh, that man can pray!" And we have thought he is a Christian, and we have been disappointed afterwards, for his life was not like his prayer.

We have sometimes heard ourselves pray, and we have thought that God has helped. Yet afterwards, we felt that our prayer showed only half the life, because there was another half. But ah! The Searcher of hearts never makes a mistake. The Searcher of hearts searches the divine life of every breath of the Spirit.

Child of God, give yourself up to the Holy Spirit to pray even when you feel you can say little. And He that searcheth the hearts knows what the mind of the Spirit is. And why? It says, "Because He maketh intercession for the saints." Note the words *for the saints*. I quoted this morning the words of Paul: "*With all . . . supplication for all saints*" (Ephesians 6: 18).

Some think that this passage does not only refer to those who are praying, but has a wider meaning, namely, that it is the Holy Spirit's one work to make supplication for all saints. Therefore, if you want this power of the Holy Spirit to pray, you must not confine Him to one saint—to yourself merely—or you will lose a great deal. You must take Him for what He is given for—to make supplications and intercession for *all saints*. Unite yourself to Him, and let Him unite Himself to you, and give yourself to make intercession for all saints.

The Holy Spirit prays within us, and God searches the heart, and there is nothing that God delights to find so much as love to all His children. I pray that you will make a study of that. Suppose you hear of a ritualist, the inclination is to condemn him. You stand at the very opposite pole and think how he may be destroying the religious life of some. But oh! *Remember to pray for him.* You may hear a man—a child of God—speak, but of whom you think: "He is not in my view sound of doctrine," and you utter a sharp word about him. But

I pray you, *pray for him*. If there is one in your circle who has grieved you, *love and pray for him*. Make intercession.

Need I remind you that the thought is a very wonderful one. Christ sits as a King upon the throne. Yes, and what is the work of a king? To rule, and to have honor and power and dominion. And Christ has that. But with all that—upon his kingly throne—He ever lives to pray. If some king on earth spent all his free time in praying for his subjects, how the sound of the piety and godliness of that man would go abroad! But oh! Our King's great work is to pray. And His great object in sending down the Holy Spirit into our hearts is that we should pray with Him.

Christians! How much of your life have you given up to intercession? Or how little? God knows. There is not one in this hall who has not reason to blush at the fact. God forgive us! And God, work a change by your almighty grace. And God, strengthen everyone who is trying to learn how to pray.

Someone in a note expressed hope that this would be "a day with Christ in the school of prayer." God grant it! Oh, that our great Intercessor and High Priest might condescend to breathe upon us, and to touch us, and to draw us, and to link us with Himself in prayer! But He can only do it as our hearts are given up to the Holy Spirit.

Let me conclude by pointing out what work we have to do this afternoon. We very definitely want to intercede for London. May God bless every prayer union that binds His children together to cry to Him. But we want something more. Oh, that without any union and without any organization, all God's children could learn: I am anointed with the Holy Spirit—that Spirit of intercession—that I may do my work!

What is the reason for the feeble Christianity in the world? What is the reason that so many souls here complain of lack of power and joy? It is this: the selfishness of our religion.

We have come to Christ to be saved, and that is the chief thing. Then there follows a little intercession and a little work in addition to the rest. We must come around to an entirely different position. We must say, "I have been redeemed to be a member of Christ's body, and like Christ, to live holy and be a blessing to the world; and like Christ, to communicate God's love to my fellow men." But you cannot do that without giving up yourself entirely to Him.

God be praised for every child of His whose eyes have been opened to see it, and whose heart has been stirred to make the blessed choice: "Yes Lord, everything, every breath, that your name may be exalted!" God be praised for every child of His in whose heart this afternoon there is the consciousness: "That has not been my life, but I am going to live it. God help me!"

But we not only want to pray for London, we want to take a little time for further intercession: to plead especially for God's children. I cannot press upon you too earnestly to pray for *all* saints. In the interval, it was suggested that we should have an All Saints Prayer Union. We do not want a new organization, by any means, but it may be that God will lead us in that direction, and you may hear about it later. But I charge you to bear the state of the Christian Church before God in Heaven as your life's work. Live to pray. You pray for your work, your circle, and for your interests—and I praise God for it. Pray for these, and not less. But pray first and pray most—in the power of the Spirit of intercession—for *all* saints. Pray for every believer in the world, for that will fill your hearts with love.

Pray for every believer you know to be wrong, or doing something wrong, or you think might be doing something wrong. You cannot pray long for a man without beginning to love him and to be humbled before the Lord. May God pour out His Spirit! May God teach us what it means that the Holy Spirit is the Spirit of intercession!

Oh, beloved! For many years you have heard more than one address and appeal about the baptism of the Holy Spirit, or you have read about it. You have heard appeals about being filled with the Spirit, about being led by the Spirit, about walking in the Spirit. But remember, the Spirit is the Spirit of intercession for *all* saints. You cannot have Him to yourself. He is the Spirit of the body.

Today, let us do two things: On the one side, let us give ourselves up to the Holy Spirit as the Spirit of intercession to pray in us, and let us say that we desire to live for God and for His Church. On the other side—in our prayers continually and in our life—let this thought be our joy and our strength: "However ignorant I feel, and however feeble my words have been, the Spirit prays in me" And God who searches the heart, knows the mind of the Spirit.

***

Sermon 3: With Wings as Eagles

But they that wait upon the LORD shall renew their strength; they shall mount up with wings as eagles; they shall run, and not be weary; and they shall walk, and not faint. (Isaiah 40: 31)

The subject announced for this evening is *Working and Waiting*. All that we have been asking God to do must manifest itself in new work. Those who have never worked cannot have been in earnest this morning when asking God to honor them with the indwelling of His heavenly love—not if they are going to live selfish lives. They cannot have been honest when they prayed the prayer: "O God, let your own, blessed love fill me, and then I will spend it, give it out; and scatter the blessing."

And those who have been working—oh, how conscious they are of the feebleness of their work! And as some may work less with great advantage, it is not always more work that is needed. The main thing is the quality of the work that is done.

This afternoon we prayed for God's mercy upon London, the workers in London, and for grace that every one of us might go out to live in the power of God's strength and love. It is hardly needful that I should speak much to you about the secret of strength for work. That is what we all need. As God's children, a divine strength is promised and prepared for us,. But how many are conscious of it? They do not know the way to receive it. And just as that one word *work* means so much earthward and manward, so the word *wait* means everything Godward. And if your work towards men is to bring blessing, it will depend entirely upon your waiting upon God.

Listen to the words of my text: "They that wait upon the Lord will renew their strength" *every day*; "they shall run and" *never* "be weary; they shall walk and not faint." Blessed life! To work, work, work, sometimes in weariness of body and of mind, sometimes in despair and failure, and yet never to be weary in spirit, and always to be carried on in the joy of God— what a kind Master! You can see that He cares for His servants, and that they are children and heirs of God. And will God allow them to be weary in spirit? Never! Especially, if they will come and dwell with Him as He is ready to have them. They that wait upon the Lord will renew their faith and shall always be strong for work.

Would God, that I had known that when I was a young minister! Would God, that I knew it even fully tonight! I thank Him for what He has shown me of it. But Oh, that He might reveal fully to my soul—and to every soul here—that they that wait upon the Lord, their strength shall always be new: "*they shall run and not be weary; they shall walk, and not faint.*"! How many are fainthearted in their work, and stop working, or work wearily, or work very little, or work with effort and struggle? And all because they do not know the joy of the Lord. May God teach us tonight how to work.

Let me take this one expression first: "They that wait upon the Lord shall renew their strength; they shall mount up with wings as eagles."

I'm sure most of you have heard sermons preached on that text or read expositions of it. But just let me give you two or three very simple thoughts about the mounting up on eagle wings.

You know the eagle is called the king of the birds, and it is said to fly the highest of all the birds, and to go straight towards the sun. And this king of birds is taken to be the image of God's children. Why? What are eagles' wings for? To carry the king of birds high up into the heavens.

Dear Christian! You are a heavenly man or woman, and are to lead a heavenly life. Your place is in the heavenlies. And how can you rise to heaven unless you have eagle wings to mount with? But, thank God! If He created the eagles with their wings to rise heavenward, He can give me eagle wings so that I too can rise upward. Yes, the believer is to live a heavenly life. His home is within the veil, in the Holist of All. He is to walk on "high places." He is to live in the love of God unclouded. He is to live with the joy of Heaven in his heart. He is to live a life in which the will of God is done as in Heaven, so on earth. The Christian needs eagle wings. But, alas! How many Christians are bound and weighed down here below!

Once when I was in Switzerland, I saw an eagle—a splendid bird—but it was chained to a rock. It had some twenty or thirty feet of chain attached to its legs and to an iron bolt in the rock. And there was the king of birds—who was meant to soar up to heaven—chained down to earth.

That is a picture of multitudes of believers. Is that your life? Are you just dragging along in the Christian life? Are you a child of God? That eagle was a king of birds, a noble king, but something kept it down. Are you allowing business, the cares of the world, the flesh to chain you down so that you cannot rise up? God forbid it should be so. I invite every believer to say tonight, "God help me to mount up on eagle wings. I want to live the heavenly life." God help us!

And then you ask me: "How can I get these eagle wings?"

I answer: "How did the eagle get its wings? By its birth. It was born a royal eagle. It had a royal descent."

Every child of God is born with eagle wings. But, alas! They do not know it. And, alas! It is not sufficiently preached. And, alas! The realization of it is not sufficiently sought from God. We are all born with eagle wings and have within us a divine nature and the very Spirit of Christ Jesus to draw us heavenward. But there are many believers who do not know they have the Spirit of Heaven within them, and many who barely know it. There are many who have an inkling of it, but are unfaithful and turn away to the world again. Oh, Christian! I tell everyone of you tonight: You have a divine nature, you have a heavenly nature, and God means you to live a heavenly life.

And then you tell me: "I have these eagle wings, but have never learnt to use them. How can I learn to use them?"

I will give you the answer. You have heard it before, perhaps, but listen once again. In Deuteronomy 32:11-12, Moses tells us how just as the eagle soars up to its nest and flutters over its young, and carries them on its back, so God carried Israel. What does that mean? Look at yonder precipice of cliffs a thousand feet high at the side of the sea. Up yonder on a ledge of rock there is an eagle's nest, and the little birds have just hatched. Come another day, and what do you see? The nest is nothing but a number of sticks gathered together and laid across. And there are the little eaglets.

The mother eagle comes and stirs up her nest with her beak and claw and scatters it. Then, what does she do? The little eaglets have looked over the cliff, and have seen the deep sea down below, and are afraid. The mother, however, casts them over so that they go fluttering about and threaten to fall and drown. But see how she hangs over them, goes in under them, stretches her broad wings and catches first the one then the other, and carries them on her back to a place of safety. God made the eagle with that instinct, and that is nothing but a picture of God's own heart.

How does God teach His eaglet children to use their wings? He comes and stirs up their nest. How does He do that? Sometimes with a trying providence, with a death, with sickness, with loss, with some tribulation, and with temptation. And why? Just as those eaglets, ready to sink, find the mother coming under them and carrying them, so the Everlasting Arms are stretched out underneath the soul that feels ready to perish. God calls upon the soul to trust Him. And just as the eaglet trusts the mother to carry it, so my God asks me to trust Him to bear me. The mother bears the little eaglet time and time again, so that it begins to take courage to soar forth, because it has learnt to use its wings. The mother taught it. And my God longs to teach His children to mount up on eagle wings.

But how can I mount up on eagle wings?

It says, "*They that **wait** upon the L*ORD *shall . . . mount up with wings as eagles.*" Yes, God often comes to the Christian worker and stirs up his nest, because He sees the eagle wings are not being used. God finds a worker very earnest, and perhaps for a time there has been blessing, but somehow self-will and the power of the flesh have come in. He has trusted in himself, so God comes and stirs up his nest.

The question now comes to the Christian worker: "What is this? Have I served my God as I might have done, or have I sinned against Him?" Then His blessed Word comes with a message, to this effect, "No, your Father loves you, but there is one thing He misses about you. You are not heavenly enough. You have worked hard, and you have worked well, and you have worked successfully, but the tenderness and the beauty of the heavenly love of Jesus are too little seen in you. The Father wants you to mount up on eagle wings. Your fellowship with your God is not as tender as it ought to be, and God has stirred and broken up your nest."

The worker is now all dark and anxious, and fears that everything will perish. He no longer finds the power he once had. Praise God! If you just learn to see that God wants you to trust Him more—to come into close union with himself.

Beloved Christian! Listen to God's Word: "*They that wait upon the Lord shall renew their strength.*" They shall go on from strength to strength. They shall get stronger month by month and year by year. They shall renew their strength and mount up with eagle wings. God help us to believe it and say tonight, "That is going to be my lot—a life mounting up on eagle wings." Does everyone dare to say that? Yes, if you dare say, "My life shall be one of waiting upon God."

What is the characteristic of eagle wings?

To be able to mount up to the heavens, the wings of the eagle must have greater strength than the wings of any other bird. And God wants His children to be strong enough that they can live above the world, so they can show the men of the world: "I am living in another world." The great mark of a disciple that Christ spoke of in His prayer to the Father was: "*They are not of the world even as I am not of the world*" (John 17: 16). They belong to Heaven as their life and heart are there.

Oh, Christian! Do believe that in your business in the city of London, in a house full of care and anxiety, you can live a heavenly life in the peace and love and joy of God. The eagle's wings are strong wings that can resist the gravitation and attraction of earth. They can rise heavenward. Praise God! *We* can live heavenly lives.

Just look how this idea of strength is the great idea of our text, and how you have it in the words that precede it: "Hast thou not known? hast thou not heard, that the everlasting God, the LORD, the Creator of the ends of the earth, fainteth not, neither is weary? There is no searching of his understanding. He giveth power to the faint; and to them that have no might he increaseth strength" (Isaiah 40: 28-29). Let me ask you weary worker. Have you heard it? Have you known that the everlasting God is never weary? You tell me, "Of course I have known it." Then believe it in the application God makes.

You ask me: "What is this application?"

The application is that if the everlasting God is never weary, *you* need never be weary, because your God is your strength. That is what the Bible teaches. You have no strength but what God gives. And you can have all the strength that God can give.

Have you heard it weary worker? Have you heard it Christian who fears that you can work but little? Have you heard it earnest intercessor who fears that the blessing will not come as you desire? Listen! "Hast thou not heard, that the everlasting God, the LORD, the Creator of the ends of the earth, fainteth not, neither is weary?" Oh! Think of that!

You find the word *faint* four times in Isaiah 40:28-31. First, it is God who *fainteth not*. Then it is "He giveth power to the *faint*," followed by "The youths shall *faint* and be weary." All human strength shall faint and be of no avail. Then finally, "*They shall run, and not be weary; and they shall walk, and not faint.*" I pray you, understand this wonderful teaching. There is the everlasting and almighty One, and you are asked to look at Him with His mighty, creative power and His power in providence.

This evening, I read the verse: "*Lift up your eyes on high, and behold who hath created these things, that bringeth out their host by number: he calleth them all by names by the greatness of his might, for that he is strong in power; not one faileth*" (Isaiah 40: 26). Every star is made to preach to you that God cares for it, and that God's power upholds it. And God's power upholds you much more, child of God. Oh! That we might begin to believe tonight in the power of almighty God! May God grant that I should believe in it fully. My heart longs to do so.

If there is one lesson we need to learn, it is the lesson of our impotence.

When I was studying and learning to be a Christian as a young man, I was told a great deal about my want of righteousness, and about my absolute worthlessness. And I believed it, and believe it still. I have no righteousness before God in myself. But I was never taught that just as little righteousness as I have, so just as little strength I have. That just as much as I am dependent on the righteousness of Christ alone for salvation, so I am also dependent on the strength of God alone for sanctification. I was not taught that, and that is the truth of God. At least, it was not taught clearly enough so as to enter my heart. It may have been my fault, but since that time, I have found so many who have not been taught it.

If you are to live holy lives and work for God, you must learn that your only hope for being holy and working in the proper way is through the everlasting God in Heaven.

Then follows the promise: "*He giveth power to the faint; and to them that have not might he increaseth strength*" (Isaiah 40: 29). God offers himself to be the power and the strength and the might of every one of His children, Oh! Is that not what we need in all our religious work—to get to that secret place of God's power, so that it can work in us?

You ask: "How can I get that power?"

Listen to the glorious answer: "They that *wait upon the* LORD shall renew their strength; they shall mount up with wings as eagles." Where do I get the power to use eagle wings, to mount and soar and rise higher and higher? *In waiting upon God.*

There are people who cannot understand that. One beloved brother in the ministry asked me last week in connection with our meetings, "Is there not a danger of too great a passivity?" I said, "Oh, yes, my brother. As long as we think it is *our* activity that must do it, then passivity robs us of time and strength. But once I understand that it is *God* who must work in us, then I realize that my highest passivity will be my highest activity. For when I give myself entirely away to God for Him to work in me, then I can work as 'they that wait upon the Lord.'"

Let us now consider what this waiting on the Lord means.

I want to disclose it to you as my parting word. When I came to Exeter Hall six months ago, we had a breakfast attended by a company of about a hundred and twenty friends. I spoke on that occasion, and gave one of the simplest messages to point out that *waiting upon God* is the one thing the Church needs. I have been perfectly surprised to find what a response that simple word has created in the hearts of God's children. And so I give you that word tonight: "*They that wait upon the Lord shall renew their strength.*"

What is needed to live such a life? My answer is first of all: If you are to wait aright upon the Lord, you must learn to know Him. You must turn away your thoughts and eyes and heart and trust from everything else, and set them upon God alone. My conduct in waiting for a man, or waiting on him, will depend entirely on what I think of Him.

But listen again. How does God reveal himself when He calls upon us to wait upon Him? You have heard the words that I have read to point us to Him as the almighty Creator. They tell us that just as His omnipotence created the world and is a guarantee for its maintenance, so the omnipotence of God is a guarantee for the strength of our Christian life. Oh! Take time to take it in. The almighty God is with me to work in my heart all that He wants me to have. Is that true? Is God's omnipotence ready to work in me all that He expects of me? There is not a doubt about it, because *I* cannot work it. And He does not ask it of me, except as He offers to work it.

Let me look at the omnipotence of God and then at His faithfulness. He is never weary and has kept the world going all these ages. Will my God then not care for me and maintain my short life of sixty, seventy or eighty years? When I look at what he does for the stars, I realize that His work is done every moment. If He withdrew His hand for one moment, the stars would fall. And God, in His omnipotence and faithfulness, is willing to work in my heart every moment of the day.

Moment by moment I'm kept in His love,
Moment by moment I've life from above,
Looking to Jesus till glory doth shine,
Moment by moment, O Lord I am Thine.

Do I keep my property—say my watch—moment by moment? And don't you think, Christian, that your God will keep you every moment? He will, if you will let Him. You are invited by Him to come and day by day to wait upon what your God is going to do for you—to expect it from Him, to look to Him in confidence, and in the blessed assurance that He will do it all. Make this the chief exercise of your religious life.

Are there any earnest Christians here tonight whose lives are not yet in the bright light of God's countenance? Let me speak a single word again to you about the blessedness of living in Christ moment by moment. This very afternoon, I was approached by a young lady who wrote me a letter last week. I will tell you the story she told me in her letter, which she confirmed this afternoon. At the meetings in Whitechapel, on the evening we spoke about absolute surrender, she wrote how she approved, understood and accepted each word, until it came to the last, when the question was asked: "Will you now absolutely surrender?" Then her fears got the better of her, and she went away very miserable.

She came again next morning, and afternoon, and evening. At the evening meeting we spoke about the omnipotence of God: "The things that are impossible with men are possible with God." She fixed her eye upon Jesus and she thought: "If that is true, Christ will strengthen me." She had the power at once to make a joyful surrender. She then wrote me how three days later she was able to prove that surrender in an act of obedience to God's voice.

Are there any of you who have not yet found the secret of a life in the full joy of Jesus' countenance and love all the day? Come tonight, and claim His omnipotence to work it in you. Let the exchange be clear. God has given you all things in Christ—all spiritual blessing, all strength, all wisdom, everything in Him. You have been holding back; you have been afraid; you have perhaps been ignorant, and have never understood it. Come tonight and say: "Absolute surrender! Lord Jesus, you shall have everything." Then trust in Him. Trust in His omnipotence to work in you all that God would have. *"They that **wait** upon the Lord shall renew their strength."*

Count upon the fact that as you go out tonight and tomorrow, you need never maintain by effort what you have got, or what has been given to you. Rather, in childlike abandonment and simple faith, say, "I am counting upon God to work it all in me." Take this word tonight: "*They that* **wait** *upon the Lord shall renew their strength.*" That is the life of power and joy!

I have said that the first thing we need to live a life of waiting upon God is *to know God upon whom we wait* and to study to know Him.

The second thing we need to know is to know ourselves.

We need to be willing and determined to accept what God reveals about us. And what does God reveal in contrast with His great omnipotence? Our utter impotence. I said a little while ago that many people believe they have no righteousness, yet they believe they have strength. But accept the word tonight: "*He giveth power to the faint; and to them that have no might he increaseth strength*" (Isaiah 40: 29). What a contrast! To a man with no might and power, God increaseth strength. But if a man has a little power, God does not do it.

Don't you see that the great secret of a right waiting upon God is to be brought down to utter impotence? I cannot repeat these words by the blessed Son of God too often: "*I do nothing of myself*" (John 8: 28). What a mystery! Jesus said that. He just waited upon God. And I ask you child of God: Wouldn't you like to occupy the very place that Jesus did before the Father and in the Father's heart? Wouldn't you be willing to take that place in order to love every day as a man who has no might, is utterly helpless, and just waits upon God?

Oh! The mischief is that we think we have so much strength and need not wait upon God. If a number of ships of war were sent out to sea, and were ready to start at any moment, and if the question were asked, "What are they waiting for?" The answer would likely be one of two things: Either they were waiting for supplies, or waiting for orders. Perhaps the stores had not been brought and they were waiting for supplies. Or else, they were waiting for orders as to what was to be done.

Child of God, that is to be your position. First of all you are to *wait for supplies.* Wait for the power of the Holy Spirit every day. Wait for the strength of God every hour. Cultivate the habit of waiting on the Lord, and your supplies will come.

Also cultivate the habit of *waiting for orders.* Wait for instruction. God is willing to teach and guide His people in a way beyond their conception. Wait for instruction. Do not think, "I have my instructions in the Bible. You often mistake them and misapply them. Study and love your Bible, but remember it is God who must give the orders, and you will fail if you take them from a book. Love your Bible and fill your heart with it, but let God apply it in your daily life.

Once more: If I am to wait upon the Lord in the proper manner, I must not only know my God, but also myself.

I must also study what this word "wait" implies.

First of all, it implies *patience.* The Bible speaks about waiting *patiently* and also about waiting *quietly.* You must cultivate that habit. How can you do it? My answer is a very simple one. I might speak it to a child or a young Christian, and yet I find older Christians who need it. I will put it this way. When you go into your closet for your morning devotions, do not—as is often done—read the Bible, think about it, pray about it, and then get up and go. But do something else in between. Before you read, set yourself still that your soul may realize: I am waiting for God to come in and take possession of me today. That is your great need.

Many a child of God spends half an hour in his private room at home. He can tell you about so many beautiful thoughts in the chapter he read, and what he prayed. But he has never got to the point where he knows that God is going to keep him all the day. And that is what you want to get in your morning prayer—an assurance from God that He will keep you. Then, you will go out into your business in the world with His strong arm about you.

Cultivate that habit before you read and in the midst of your reading. Sometimes shut your eyes and just sit quietly and say, "My God, in the midst of my reading I wait on You to make the Word living in my heart."

Then, before you pray, sit still, and shut your eyes and say, "Will God now listen to me for certain? Shall I get an answer when I pray?" Get waiting upon God and then kneel down and pray your prayer—very shortly perhaps. Say, "Am I waiting upon my God?" Then pray very definitely what you want, and let your soul grow into the blessed consciousness—not that you have fed on some beautiful words of God, not that you have prayed an earnest prayer for this and that—but let your soul go out in your quiet hour in this one consciousness: "I have been waiting upon God, and God has answered me, and God will keep me today."

Oh, learn to come into blessed fellowship with God. May you never, never pray a prayer without the blessed thought: "*As the eyes of servants look unto the hands of their masters. . . so our eyes wait upon the Lord our God*" (Psalm 123: 2). Wait quietly, wait patiently.

And then wait *continually*—not one or two days, not one moment, but all the day. Take the text in Psalm 25: 5: "*On Thee do I wait all the day.*" Pray for the Holy Spirit to bring you into that blessed habit of waiting all the day upon God to give you instruction, to guide, to order, to help, to give supplies of grace and joy and strength; and God will do it. "*Blessed are all they that wait for him*" (Isaiah 30: 18).

Our time will not allow us to speak longer, but just one more text: "*Men have not heard . . . neither hath the eye seen . . . what He hath prepared for him that waiteth for Him*" (Isaiah 64:4). Oh! Learn to look to God for unexpected things. Learn to give up your thoughts about what God can do. Rest upon His promises to you, and plead them. Then you will find that God can do beyond what you can conceive. Expect God, by the Holy Spirit, to work in you something utterly beyond your comprehension, and God will do it. "*They that wait upon the Lord shall renew their strength.*"

And now before we part, we want to spend half an hour in waiting upon God together. We want to plead with God to make us all very strong in the strength of the Lord, and to give us all eagle wings. He *has* given them to us. And if we wait upon Him, He will give us the grace to use them to mount up, and to run and not be weary, and to walk and not faint. God grant to us the spirit of waiting upon Him. For Jesus' sake. Amen.

*

About Andrew Murray

Andrew Murray was born in Graaff-Reinet on the Eastern Frontier of the Cape on 9 May 1828. His father, Andrew Murray Sr., had come to the Cape from Scotland in 1822 with a group of other Scottish ministers to help fill the many pastoral vacancies in the Dutch Reformed Church at the time.

When Andrew was ten, and his brother John, twelve, his father sent them to Aberdeen, Scotland to pursue their education. While there, they stayed with their uncle, Rev. John Murray. It was at his home that both Andrew and John were powerfully influenced by the revivalist preacher W.C. Burns.

University years in Scotland and Utrecht

In 1845, when Andrew was just 17 and his brother 19, they both gained their M.A. degrees from Marischal College, Aberdeen University. They then left for Utrecht in Holland to study theology.

When they arrived there, they befriended students who attended the Christian club, *Sechor Dabar* (Remember the Word), which had been founded in association with the *Reveil Movement* in 1843.

It was as a result of the meetings arranged by this movement that Andrew was able to write to his father on 14 November 1845 that he "had been born again." On 9 May 1849 (his twentieth birthday), he and his brother were ordained at the Hague just prior to their return to the Cape.

Bloemfontein: A time of trial and tribulation

Just three days before his twenty-first birthday, he was inducted as minister of Bloemfontein, the capital of the Orange River Sovereignty. This territory, which is situated beyond the borders of the Cape, had been annexed by Britain in 1848.

Andrew's congregation consisted of 12,000 emigrant farmers (now known as Voortrekkers) covering 50,000 square miles. In addition, he also ministered to 8000 Dutch emigrants in the vast territory across the Vaal River that later became known as the Transvaal.

It was during this period that he realized that there was no power in his preaching. He even thought of leaving the ministry. But strangely enough, after falling ill with malaria while touring the Transvaal, his calling became clear.

The outbreak of revival in 1860

In 1856, Andrew married Emma Rutherfoord (1835-1905) in Cape Town. Shortly afterwards, he became temporary rector of Grey College, a combined secondary school and teachers' college for boys.

At the end of 1859, he was called to Worcester in the Western Cape. Barely a month after his induction there on 27 May 1860, revival broke out on the farms nearby, and soon spread throughout the Winelands of the Western Cape. During a second wave in 1861, it swept throughout the Cape Colony and even reached Bloemfontein as well as a parish in the Transvaal.

These were times of great spiritual blessing for Andrew Murray. But after two years, he found that most members of his congregation had lost their conscious closeness to the Lord. This led him to write *Blijf in Jesus* in 1864.

Not long after, he found himself in a similar spiritual state to that of his congregation. Although he consecrated himself anew to the Lord, years would pass before he experienced the fruit of that consecration.

In 1862, he was elected moderator of the Dutch Reformed Synod at the age of thirty-four. As the revival was still in full swing, this Synod was expected to be one of thanksgiving and praise, but instead, it turned into a verbal battleground where pastors of a liberal hue denigrated the revival and the Bible-based theology of the orthodox pastors.

Cape Town and Wellington

In the middle of the furor over liberalism, Andrew accepted a call to the *Groote Kerk* in Cape Town in 1864. As moderator, this enabled him to be in the center of the action. After winning the battle against liberalism through lectures and sermons, he accepted a call to the small village of Wellington in 1871.

The Huguenot Teachers' Seminary

While on vacation in December 1872, he read the biography of Mary Lyon of the Ladies' Seminary at Mount Holyoke in Massachusetts, USA. Impressed by Mary Lyon's Christian vision for her student teachers, he decided to establish a similar Teachers' Training establishment in Wellington.

With the enthusiastic support of his congregation, the Huguenot Seminary was formerly opened on 19 January 1874. Its first lecturers were Abbey Park Ferguson and Anna E. Bliss, both former students of Mount Holyoke.

To raise sufficient funds for this educational project, Andrew went on an extended collection tour around the Colony. He was able to raise £2,300 in the process.

The Mission Training Institute

In October 1877, the Wellington congregation under Andrew's leadership opened the Mission Training Institute for missionaries, lay workers, and teachers of religious instruction. The focus was on attracting young men who were not sufficiently educated, or did not have the funds to attend the Theological Seminary in Stellenbosch.

The first lecturers were Rev. George Ferguson (brother of Miss Abbey Ferguson at the Huguenot Seminary) and DS. J.C. Pauw of the local Colored Missionary Church.

Church Statesman

Andrew was elected as moderator of the Cape Synod six times: 1862, 1876, 1883, 1886, 1890 and 1894. He was known as a chairman who could be firm without being obstinate, tolerant without being weak, and impartial without being unyielding.

He was awarded two honorary doctorates: one in Divinity from Aberdeen University in 1898, and one in Literature from Cape Town University in 1907.

Preacher

Andrew was a fiery, spirit-filled preacher. Those who heard him preach, describe a powerful voice issuing from a delicate frame—a prophet whose speech was like molten eloquence overflowing his audience.

Author

During his lifetime, he published no less than 250 books and tracts, with some of his major works being translated into fifteen languages. Towards the end of his life, he decided to publish a series of pocket books in which his teachings on the spiritual life is succinctly and beautifully presented. They are among the best of his works.

Missionary Statesman

Andrew's interest in missions reached new heights with the establishment of the Missions Institute in his pastorate of Wellington in 1877. It proved a huge success, resulting in its graduates establishing mission stations in Bechuanaland (Botswana), Mashonaland (Zimbabwe), Nyasaland (Malawi), Northern Rhodesia (Zambia), and the Sudan.

According to a census taken in 1927—just ten years after Murray's death—1447 schools had been established with 96,309 students and 2699 teachers. During 1927 alone, there were 304 Dutch Reformed missionaries on the field who were serving churches with 19,440 baptized members and 15 282 confirmation candidates. All in all, 72,079 Africans had been baptized in the above-mentioned countries since the establishment of mission stations there. We also do well to remember that these statistics do not cover the Dutch Reformed mission fields within South Africa itself.

Besides championing the practical side of missions, he was also interested in the theoretical side, especially the lack of motivation within the world-wide church to promote Christ's Great Commission. In 1901, he wrote *The Key to the Missionary Problem,* and in 1910 *The State of the Church.*

It goes without saying that the true extent of Andrew Murray's legacy will only be known one day in Glory.

***

If you feel that these talks have helped to deepen your walk with the Lord, please consider posting a review on Amazon or Goodreads. It will go a long way towards making Andrew Murray known to a new generation of Christian readers who may be prompted to read this book or one or other of his wonderful devotional works.

*

Other books by Olea Nel

The Destined Series:

Three novels on Andrew Murray's hectic ministry during his time in Bloemfontein (1849-1860). Available from this link: https://amzn.to/2YKCvOZ or go to Olea Nel's website for further information at www.oleanel.com

Coming in 2021:

Andrew Murray and the Cape Revival of 1860/61
Andrew Murray: From Spark to Flame

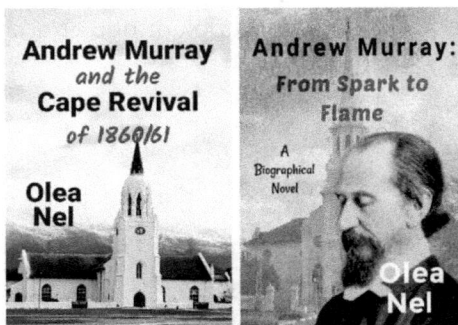

For more information, please go to Olea Nel's website at www.oleanel.com

***

www.ingramcontent.com/pod-product-compliance
Lightning Source LLC
LaVergne TN
LVHW021349080426
835508LV00020B/2194